Everyman, I will go with thee,
and be thy guide

THE EVERYMAN
LIBRARY

*The Everyman Library was founded by J. M. Dent
in 1906. He chose the name Everyman because he wanted
to make available the best books ever written in every
field to the greatest number of people at the cheapest possible
price. He began with Boswell's 'Life of Johnson';
his one-thousandth title was Aristotle's 'Metaphysics',
by which time sales exceeded forty million.*

*Today Everyman paperbacks remain true to
J. M. Dent's aims and high standards, with a wide range
of titles at affordable prices in editions which address
the needs of today's readers. Each new text is reset to give
a clear, elegant page and to incorporate the latest thinking
and scholarship. Each book carries the pilgrim logo,
the character in 'Everyman', a medieval morality play,
a proud link between Everyman
past and present.*

H. G. Wells

THE TIME MACHINE
THE CENTENNIAL EDITION

Edited by
JOHN LAWTON

EVERYMAN
J. M. DENT • LONDON
CHARLES E. TUTTLE
VERMONT

Introduction and other critical apparatus
© J.M.Dent 1995

Text copyright by the Literary Executors
of the Estate of H. G. Wells

All rights reserved

First published by J. M. Dent in Everyman's Library 1935
Reissued 1992
New Edition 1993
Reprinted 1994 (twice)
New Centennial Edition 1995
Reprinted 1996 (twice)

J. M. Dent
Orion Publishing Group
Orion House
5 Upper St Martin's Lane,
London WC2H 9EA
and
Charles E. Tuttle Co. Inc
28 South Main Street,
Rutland, Vermont 05701, USA

Typeset by CentraCet Limited, Cambridge
Printed in Great Britain by
The Guernsey Press Co. Ltd, Guernsey, C.I.

This book if bound as a paperback is subject to
the condition that it may not be issued on loan or otherwise
except in its original binding

British Library Cataloguing-in-Publication Data
available on request

ISBN 0 460 87735-6

The editor and publishers wish to thank the following for
permission to use copyright material: J. M. Dent/Everyman's
Library for material from Michael Moorcock, 'Introduction'
to *The Time Machine*, 1993; David Higham Associates on
behalf of the author for material from Vincent Brome, *H. G.
Wells: A Biography*, Longmans, 1952; Peters Fraser &
Dunlop Group Ltd on behalf of the author for material from
J. B. Priestley, 'Introduction' to *War of the Worlds*, Easton
Press, 1964; Random House UK Ltd for material from
Raymond Williams, *The English Novel from Dickens*, Chatto
& Windus, 1974.
Every effort has been made to trace all the copyright holders
but if any have been inadvertently overlooked the publishers
will be pleased to make the necessary arrangement at the first
opportunity.

CONTENTS

NOTE ON THE AUTHOR AND EDITOR

H. G. WELLS was born in Bromley, Kent in 1866. After working as a draper's apprentice and pupil-teacher, he won a scholarship to the Normal School of Science, South Kensington, in 1884, studying under T. H. Huxley. He was awarded a first-class honours degree in biology and resumed teaching, but had to retire after a kick from an ill-natured pupil, at football, afflicted his kidneys. He worked in poverty in London as a crammer while experimenting in journalism and stories, and published textbooks on biology and physiography (1893), but it was *The Time Machine* (1895) that launched his literary career. Many scientific romances and short stories began to be paralleled with sociological and political books and tracts, notably *Anticipations* (1901), *Mankind in the Making* (1903), *A Modern Utopia* (1905). His full-length, largely autobiographical novels began with *The Wheels of Chance* (1896), *Love and Mr Lewisham* (1900), *Kipps* (1905), *Tono-Bungay* and *Ann Veronica* (1909), the last promoting the outspoken, socially and sexually liberated 'New Woman'. He married his cousin Isabel in 1891, but later eloped with, and subsequently married, Catherine Robbins, 'Jane'. A constant philanderer, he invited scandal by including his lightly concealed private affairs in *Ann Veronica* and *The New Machiavelli* (1911). Shaw and the Webbs had invited him into the Fabian Society and soon regretted it. Wells increasingly used fiction as a platform for the ideas and visions of a world-state which preoccupied him, but he foresaw that the novel itself would decline to be replaced by candid autobiography. After about 1920, critical attention was turning towards his natural successors Aldous Huxley and George Orwell, and the 'pure' non-journalistic novels of James Joyce and Virginia Woolf.

Further information about Wells can be obtained from the H. G. Wells Society, 75 Wellmeadow Road, London SE13 9TA.

JOHN LAWTON was born in Derbyshire. Over the last ten years he has worked for several London publishing firms, produced forty-odd programmes for Channel 4, written a socio-political history of the Kennedy–Macmillan years, worked as a film reviewer, edited a reissue of G. K. Chesteron and written a novel, *Black Out* (Weidenfeld, 1994). He has just completed films on the USA with Gore Vidal and Scott Turow.

CHRONOLOGY OF WELLS'S LIFE

Year	Life
1866	Born 21 September, Bromley, Kent, to a working class family: father a gardener, shopkeeper and cricketer; mother a maid and housekeeper
1873	Entered Thomas Morley's Bromley Academy

CHRONOLOGY OF HIS TIMES

Year	Arts & Science	History & Politics
1865	Mendel's *Law of Heredity*	End of American Civil War; Lincoln assassinated
1866	Dostoevsky's *Crime and Punishment*	Russia defeated Austria at Sadowa
1867	Ibsen's *Peer Gynt*; Lister experiments with sterile surgery	Dominion of Canada founded
1868	Browning's *The Ring and the Book*; typewriter first patented	Gladstone Prime Minister
1869	Jules Verne's *20,000 Leagues Under the Sea*; Flaubert's *Education Sentimentale*; John Stuart Mill's *On the Subjection of Women*	Suez Canal opened
1870	Charles Dickens dies; T. H. Huxley's *Theory of Biogenesis*	Franco-Prussian War; Prussia defeats France at Sedan; fall of Napoleon III; Education Act, introducing elementary education for 5–13 year olds
1871	Lewis Carroll's *Alice Through the Looking Glass*; George Eliot's *Middlemarch*; Charles Darwin's *The Descent of Man*	Paris Commune suppressed; the Chicago Fire; unification of Germany
1872	Edison's duplex telegraph	The Secret Ballot Act
1873	Tolstoy's *Anna Karenina*; James Clarke Maxwell's *Electricity and Magnetism*	Napoleon III dies in exile in Kent; David Livingstone dies in what is now Zambia
1874	Thomas Hardy's *Far from the Madding Crowd*; first Impressionist exhibition in Paris	Disraeli Prime Minister; Factory Act introduces fifty-six and a half hour week
1875	Bizet's *Carmen*	London Medical School for Women founded
1876	Alexander Graham Bell's telephone; Twain's *Tom Sawyer*	Battle of Little Bighorn; death of General Custer; Queen Victoria becomes Empress of India

Year   *Life*

1880   Apprenticed to Rodgers and Benyer, Drapers, at Windsor

1881   Pupil-teacher at Alfred Williams' school at Wookey, Somerset;
         pupil at Midhurst Grammar School; apprenticed to Southsea
         Drapery Emporium

1883–4   Under-master at Midhurst Grammar School; wins scholarship
         and bursary at Normal School of Science, South Kensington

1884–7   Studies under T. H. Huxley at the Normal School of Science;
         begins to write; first published work appears in May 1887 in the
         Science Schools Journal – *A Tale of the Twentieth Century*

1887   Aged 20; teacher at Holt Academy, Wrexham

1888   Returns to London after illness, working as a teacher; *The
         Chronic Argonauts* published in Science Schools Journal

1890   B.Sci degree

1891   Tutor for University Correspondence College; marries his
         cousin, Isabel Wells; *The Rediscovery of the Unique* published in
         the Fortnightly Review

Year	Arts & Science	History & Politics
1877	Thomas Edison's phonograph	Britain annexes the Transvaal
1879	Dostoevsky's *The Brothers Karamazov*	Zulu Wars, South Africa
1880	Electric light devised by T. A. Edison (USA) and by J. W. Swan (Scotland)	Boer uprising in the Transvaal
1881	Henry James's *Portrait of a Lady*	President Garfield murdered, USA
1882	R. L. Stevenson's *Treasure Island*	Married Woman's Property Act
1883	Death of Karl Marx; William Thomson (later, Lord Kelvin) publishes *On the Size of Atoms*; first skyscraper in Chicago	Fabian Society founded
1884	Twain's *Huckleberry Finn*; invention of Maxim machine gun	Berlin Conference on division of Africa; Gladstone's Reform Act extends vote to country householders
1885	Zola's *Germinal*; Pasteur's vaccine to cure hydrophobia; Karl Benz's automobile	Battle of Khartoum; Death of General Gordon
1886	R. L. Stevenson's *Dr Jekyll and Mr Hyde*; Rimbaud's *Les Illuminations*	Lord Salisbury Prime Minister
1887	H. W. Goodwin's celluloid film invented; speed of light measured	Queen Victoria's Golden Jubilee
1888	Kipling's *Plain Tales from the Hills*; Eastman's box camera; Dunlop's pneumatic tyre; Hertz discovers electromagnetic waves	Kaiser Frederick III dies after only three months as Emperor of Germany; accession of Wilhelm II
1889	Death of Robert Browning; T. H. Huxley's *Agnosticism*; Eiffel Tower built	Archduke Rudolf, heir to the Emperor, commits suicide at Mayerling, Austria
1890	Emily Dickinson's *Poems*; discovery of tetanus and diptheria viruses	Bismarck dismissed by the Kaiser; the 'O'Shea' scandal; Charles Parnell resigns as leader of Irish party
1891	Wilde's *The Picture of Dorian Gray*; Hardy's *Tess of the D'Urbervilles*	

Year	Life
1892	Meets Amy Catherine Robbins – 'Jane'
1893	Elopes with Jane; in poor health; first published book, *A Text Book of Biology*; lives by writing for the rest of his life
1895	Aged 27; marries Jane; they settle in Woking; meets George Bernard Shaw; *The Time Machine*; *Select Conversations with an Uncle*; *The Wonderful Visit*; *The Stolen Bacillus*
1896	Aged 30; *The Island of Doctor Moreau*; *The Wheels of Chance*; meets George Gissing
1897	*The Invisible Man*; *The Plattner Story and Others*; *Thirty Strange Stories*; *The Star*
1898	In poor health again; travels to Italy; meets Edmund Gosse, Henry James, Joseph Conrad, J. M. Barrie; *The War of the Worlds*
1899	*When the Sleeper Wakes*; *Tales of Space and Time*
1900	Aged 34; now rich enough to have house built at Sandgate, Kent; *Love and Mr Lewisham*
1901	*Anticipations*; *The First Men in the Moon*; birth of first son 'Gip', G. P. Wells

Year	Arts & Science	History & Politics
1892	Kipling's *Barrack Room Ballads*; Diesel's internal combustion engine	Keir Hardie wins first seat in Parliament for Labour (ILP)
1893	Henry Ford's first automobile	Gladstone's Irish Home Rule Bill defeated
1894	Shaw's *Arms and the Man*; Edison's Kinetoscope Parlour, New York; Emile Berliner's gramophone disc	Death of Alexander III, Tsar of Russia; accession of Nicholas II
1895	Conrad's *Almayer's Folly*; Freud's *Studies in Hysteria*; Wilhelm Rontgen introduces X-rays; Gillette's safety razor.	Hispano–Cuban war; London School of Economics founded; Jameson Raid, South Africa
1896	Chekhov's *The Seagull*; Nobel Prizes instituted; William Ramsay discovers helium. Rutherford publishes researches into magnetic detection of electrical waves; Becquerel determines radioactivity of uranium	Cecil Rhodes resigns as PM of Cape Colony
1897	Shaw's *Candida*; The Webbs's *Industrial Democracy*; Havelock Ellis's *Studies in the Psychology of Sex*; Robert Ross discovers the cause of malaria; Marconi's first radio transmission	Queen Victoria's Diamond Jubilee; Indian revolt on North West Frontier
1898	Zola's *J'Accuse*; Wilde's *The Ballad of Reading Gaol*; Henry James's *The Turn of the Screw*; the Curies discover radium	Cuban–American War; death of Bismarck; Battle of Omdurman, Sudan; General Kitchener retakes Khartoum
1899	Wilde's *The Importance of Being Earnest*	Dreyfus pardoned; Boer War begins
1900	Conrad's *Lord Jim*; Chekhov's *Uncle Vanya*; Freud's *The Interpretation of Dreams*; Planck's Quantum Theory; deaths of Ruskin and Wilde	Boxer Rebellion in China
1901	Kipling's *Kim*; Thomas Mann's *Buddenbrooks*; Marconi transmits radio communication across the Atlantic	Assassination of President McKinley, USA; Theodore Roosevelt succeeds; Queen Victoria dies; accession of Edward VII

Year	Life
1902	*The Sea Lady*; *The Discovery of the Future*
1903	Joins Fabian Society, the Coefficients, and the Reform Club; birth of second son, Frank; *Twelve Stories and a Dream*; *Mankind in the Making*
1904	*The Food of the Gods*
1905	Aged 39; *Kipps*; *A Modern Utopia*
1906	Affairs with Amber Reeves and Rosamund Bland; meets Gorky in New York; *In the Days of the Comet*; *Socialism and the Family*; *The Future in America*; *This Misery of Boots*; *The So-called Science of Sociology*
1908	Resigns from the Fabians; *First and Last Things*; *The War in the Air*; *New Worlds for Old*
1909	Birth of Wells's daughter, Anna, to Amber Reeves; Wells and Jane move to Hampstead; *Tono-Bungay*; *Ann Veronica*
1910	Aged 44; *The History of Mr Polly*

Year	Arts & Science	History & Politics
1902	Conrad's *Heart of Darkness*; Bennett's *Anna of the Five Towns*; William James's *The Varieties of Religious Experience*; Caruso's first record	End of the Boer War
1903	The Wright Brothers succeed in powered flight; Henry Ford starts Ford Motors; Samuel Butler's *The Way of All Flesh*; Shaw's *Man & Superman*	Bolshevik–Menshevik split in Russian socialists; Lenin becomes Bolshevik leader
1904	Picasso's *The Two Sisters*; Freud's *The Psychopathology of Everyday Life*; Chekhov's *The Cherry Orchard*	Russo–Japanese War begins; Theodore Roosevelt re-elected
1905	Einstein's Special Theory of Relativity; Debussy's *La Mer*; Cézanne's *Les Grandes Baigneuses*; Edith Wharton's *House of Mirth*; Shaw's *Major Barbara* forbidden by New York police	Russia defeated by Japan; riots in St Petersburg, 'the Potemkin' mutinies
1906	J. J. Thompson wins Nobel Prize for Physics	American occupation of Cuba; Liberal victory in General Election – maj. 218; Labour win 54 seats
1907	First Cubist exhibition in Paris; Kipling's Nobel Prize for Literature; Conrad's *The Secret Agent*	Defeat of Labour bill to give votes to women; arrest of fifty-seven suffragettes in London
1908	Arnold Bennett's *The Old Wives' Tale*; E. M. Forster's *A Room with a View*; Rutherford wins Nobel Prize for Physics; Wright Brothers tour Europe	Asquith Prime Minister; Mrs Pankhurst imprisoned
1909	Diaghilev's Russian Ballet in Paris; Peary Expedition at North Pole; Bleriot flies the Channel	Murderer Dr Crippen arrested
1910	Marie Curie's *Treatise on Radiography*; Stravinsky's *Firebird*; Roger Fry's Post–Impressionist Exhibition in London; E. M. Forster's *Howards End*; Tolstoy dies	Death of Edward VII; accession of George V

Year	Life
1911	*The New Machiavelli*; *The Country of the Blind and Other Stories*; *Floor Games* (for children); moves to Easton Glebe, Essex
1912	Meets Rebecca West; *Marriage*
1913	*The Passionate Friends*; *Little Wars*
1914	Birth of Wells's son, Anthony, to Rebecca West; visits Russia with Maurice Baring; *The Wife of Sir Isaac Harman*; *The World Set Free*; *An Englishman Looks at the World*; *The War That Will End War*
1915	*Boon* (originally published under the pseudonym Reginald Bliss); break with Henry James; *The Research Magnificent*; *Bealby*
1916	Aged 50; visits Western Front in France and Italy; *Mr Britling Sees it Through*; *The Elements of Reconstruction*; *What is Coming?*
1917	*The Soul of a Bishop*; *Wars and the Future*; *God, the Invisible King*
1918	*Joan and Peter*; joins Ministry of Information under Lord Northcliffe
1919	*The Undying Fire*; *History is One*; contributor to *The Idea of a League of Nations*

Year	Arts & Science	History & Politics
1911	Amundsen at South Pole; Rutherford's *Theory of Atomic Structure*; D. H. Lawrence's *The White Peacock*; Ezra Pound's *Cantos*; Rupert Brooke's *Poems*	Lords Reform Bill passed in Lords after intervention of the King; Liberals announce first measures for National Insurance
1912	Schoenberg's *Pierrot Lunaire*; Jung's *The Theory of Psychoanalysis*	The *Titanic* disaster; Woodrow Wilson elected US President
1913	Vitamin A isolated at Yale, by Elmer McCollum; Lawrence's *Sons and Lovers*	Panama Canal opened; hunger strikes by Suffragettes in prison
1914	J. H. Jean's *Radiation and the Quantum Theory*; James Joyce's *Dubliners*	Assassination of Archduke Franz Ferdinand of Austria in Sarajevo; the Great War starts
1915	D. W. Griffith's film *Birth of a Nation*; Somerset Maugham's *Of Human Bondage*; Lawrence's *The Rainbow* banned; Joseph Conrad's *Victory*	The Allied failure at Gallipoli; Zeppelins attack London; the *Lusitania* sinking; Coalition Government formed in Britain
1916	Death of Henry James; James Joyce's *Portrait of the Artist as a Young Man*; Dadaism in Zurich	The battle of Verdun; the Easter Rising, Dublin; Battle of Jutland; President Wilson's plea for peace; Lloyd George Prime Minister
1917	Freud's *Introduction to Psychoanalysis*; T. S. Eliot's *Prufrock*	America enters the war; Russian Revolution; Lenin in power; Woodrow Wilson re-elected
1918	Matisse's *Odalisques*; Joyce's *Ulysses*	Collapse of the Central Powers ends the Great War; Versailles Peace Conference; vote given to women over thirty and men over twenty-one; first woman elected to Parliament – Countess Markiewicz (Sinn Fein)
1919	Thomas H. Morgan's *The Physical Basis of Heredity*; Thomas Hardy's *Collected Poems*; Maugham's *The Moon and Sixpence*; J. M. Keynes's *The Economic Consequences of the Peace*; Bauhaus founded; Alcock and Brown fly the Atlantic	Herbert Hoover takes control of European Relief; Prohibition in America; Versailles Treaty signed; President Wilson awarded Nobel Peace Prize; socialist uprising in Berlin crushed by troops; murder of Rosa Luxembourg

Year	Life
1920	Visits Russia; meets Lenin and Moura Budberg; *The Outline of History*; *Russia in the Shadows*
1921	Aged 55; visits USA; *The Salvaging of Civilization*
1922	*A Short History of the World*; *The Secret Places of the Heart*; unsuccessful as a Labour Parliamentary candidate for London University
1923	*Men Like Gods*; *The Story of a Great Schoolmaster*; *The Dream*; stands for Parliament again but defeated
1924	Begins affair with Odette Keun
1925	*Christina Alberta's Father*
1926	Aged 60; *The World of William Clissold*
1927	Death of Jane Wells; *Meanwhile*; *Collected Short Stories*; *Democracy Under Revision*; collected H. G. Wells (Atlantic edition)
1928	*The Open Conspiracy: Blue Prints for a World Revolution*; *Mr Blettsworthy on Rampole Island*; introduction to *The Book of Catherine Wells*

Year	Arts & Science	History & Politics
1920	Eddington's *Space, Time and Gravitation*; F. Scott Fitzgerald's *This Side of Paradise*; Sinclair Lewis's *Main Street*; Edith Wharton's *The Age of Innocence*	America rejects the League of Nations; National Socialist Workers party (NAZI) publishes manifesto, Germany
1921	Einstein wins Nobel Prize for Physics	Victory of Red Army in Russian Civil War
1922	T. S. Eliot's *The Waste Land*; first transmissions by BBC	Mussolini establishes dictatorship in Italy; Irish Free State established
1923	Gershwin's *Rhapsody in Blue*; E. N. da C. Andrade's *The Structure of the Atom*; Freud's *The Ego and the Id*; W. B. Yeats awarded Nobel Prize for Literature	Hitler's NAZI coup fails in Munich; Stanley Baldwin Prime Minister; Matrimonial Bill passed, allowing wives to divorce husbands; British Mandate in Palestine
1924	E. M. Forster's *A Passage to India*; Thomas Mann's *Magic Mountain*	Lenin dies; Minority Labour government; Ramsay MacDonald Prime Minister
1925	John Logie Baird's successful television experiments; Eisenstein's film *Battleship Potemkin*; Chaplin's *The Gold Rush*; Fitzgerald's *The Great Gatsby*	Hitler publishes *Mein Kampf*
1926	Fritz Lang's film *Metropolis*; William Faulkner's *Soldier's Pay*; Kafka's *The Castle*; Hemingway's *The Sun also Rises*; R. H. Tawney's *Religion and the Rise of Capitalism*	British troops withdraw from the Rhineland; British Commonwealth instituted; General Strike
1927	Lindbergh's flight from New York to Paris; Abel Gance's film *Napoleon*; Virginia Woolf's *The Lighthouse*; *The Jazz Singer* (first talkie); completion of Proust's *A la Recherche du Temps Perdu*	Trotsky expelled from Russian Communist Party
1928	J. L. Baird demonstrates colour TV; Eisenstein's film *October*	Vote given to women over twenty-one – equal rights; Chiang Kai-shek President of China

Year   *Life*

1929   First broadcasts on BBC; *The Autocracy Of Mr Parham*; *The Adventures of Tommy* (for children); film script of *The King Who Was a King*

1930   Moves back to London

1931   Aged 65; *The Science of Life* (A Summary of Contemporary Knowledge about Life and its Possibilities with Julian Huxley and G. P. Wells); diagnosed as diabetic; *What Are We To Do With Our Lives?*

1932   *The Bulpington of Blup*; *The Work, Wealth and Happiness of Mankind*

1933   Begins affair with Moura Budberg; *The Shape of Things to Come*

1934   Talks with Stalin and with F. D. Roosevelt; *Experiment in Autobiography*

1935   Works with Alexander Korda on film version of *The Shape of Things to Come*; *The New America*

Year	Arts & Science	History & Politics
1929	Robert Graves's *Goodbye to All That*; Hemingway's *A Farewell to Arms*; Thomas Mann wins Nobel Prize for Literature	Crash of New York Stock Exchange, Wall Street; Second Minority Labour Government; thirteen women elected to Parliament; NAZI victory in Bavarian elections
1930	Freud's *Civilization and its Discontents*; W. H. Auden's *Poems*; Robert Frost's *Collected Poems*; Sinclair Lewis wins Nobel Prize for Literature; Amy Johnson's flight from London to Australia; death of D. H. Lawrence	Haile Selassie (Ras Tafari) becomes Emperor of Ethiopia; Gandhi's Salt March, India; NAZI party becomes second largest in Germany
1931	Death of Edison; Empire State Building completed; Chaplin's *City Lights*; Schweitzer's *My Life and Thoughts*; Faulkner's *Sanctuary*	World slump begins with the collapse of the Credit Anstadt bank, Vienna; first woman elected to the American Senate; National Government, Britain
1932	James Chadwick discovers the neutron; Fritz Lang's film of Huxley's *Brave New World*; Galsworthy's Nobel Prize for Literature	Franklin D. Roosevelt wins US Presidential election; New Deal initiated; Stalin purges begin, Russia
1933	A. N. Whitehead's *Adventures of Ideas*; Jung's *Psychology and Religion*; Orwell's *Down and Out in Paris and London*	Hitler becomes Chancellor; start of anti-Jewish measures in Germany; first concentration camps; Germany leaves League of Nations
1934	Gershwin's *Porgy and Bess*; Graves's *I Claudius*	'Night of the Long Knives' massacre in Germany; Hitler assumes title of 'Führer', after plebiscite
1935	The Curies awarded Nobel Prize for Chemistry, having synthesized radioactive elements; The Webbs's *Soviet Communism; A New Civilization*; Graham Greene's *England Made Me*; T. S. Eliot's *Murder in the Cathedral*	Hitler denounces Versailles Treaty, forms Air Force and imposes conscription; Russian Show Trials; Italy invades Abyssinia

Year	Life
1936	Aged 70; awarded Hon.D.Litt by London University; *The Anatomy of Frustration*; *The Croquet Player*; *The Man Who Could Work Miracles*; *The Idea of a World Encyclopaedia*
1937	*Brynhild*; *Star Begotten*; *The Camford Visitation*
1938	*Apropos of Dolores*; *World Brain*; *The Brothers*
1939	Aged 72; visits Sweden; *The Fate Of Homo Sapiens*; *Travels of a Republican Radical In Search of Hot Water*; *The Holy Terror*
1940	In London during Blitz; speaking tour of USA; *The Commonsense of War and Peace*; *Babes in the Darkling Wood· All Abroad for Ararat*
1941	*Guide to the New World*; *You Can't be Too Careful*
1942	*Phoenix*; *Science and the World Mind*; *The Conquest of Time* (final revision of *First and Last Things*)
1943	*Crux Ansata*

Year	Arts & Science	History & Politics
1936	Chaplin's *Modern Times*; Alexander Korda's film *Things to Come*; Dylan Thomas's *Twenty-Five Poems*; Kipling, Houseman and Chesterton die; A. J. Ayer's *Language, Truth and Logic*	Hitler reoccupies the Rhineland; Spanish Civil War begins; Rome–Berlin Axis announced; death of George v; Edward VIII accedes in January, abdicates in December; 'Battle of Cable St' in London's East End
1937	Picasso's *Guernica*; Steinbeck's *Of Mice and Men*; Orwell's *The Road to Wigan Pier*; Sartre's *La Nausée*; Wallace Carothers invents Nylon	Stalin purges high Party and military officials; Japanese Imperialism in China, Peking and Shanghai captured
1938	Orson Welles's radio feature of H. G. Wells's *The War of the Worlds* terrifies America	Austria falls to Hitler; Munich Conference over Czecho-Slovakia; Appeasement Policy confirmed; Franco's victories in Spain; Roosevelt appeals to the dictators for peace
1939	Death of Freud; Jolie-Curie shows the potential of nuclear fission. Henry Moore's *Reclining Figure*; Joyce's *Finnegan's Wake*; Steinbeck's *The Grapes of Wrath*; death of Yeats, and of Ford Madox Ford	Germany invades Poland; Second World War begins; Hitler-Stalin Pact; Russia invades Finland and Poland; fall of Madrid to Franco
1940	Koestler's *Darkness at Noon*	Churchill Prime Minister; Dunkirk and collapse of France; Battle of Britain; start of Blitz on London; murder of Trotsky
1941	Welles's *Citizen Kane*; Carrol Reed's film *Kipps*	Hitler invades Russia; Japan bombs Pearl Harbor; America enters the War
1942	Evelyn Waugh's *Put Out More Flags*	Japan invades Burma, Malaya, Dutch East Indies; Singapore surrenders; Americans bomb Tokyo; Stalingrad siege begins; Montgomery wins El Alamein; start of Hitler's 'Final Solution'
1943	Henry Moore's sculpture *Madonna and Child*	Russian victory at Stalingrad; Warsaw Ghetto killings; Allies finally conquer North Africa; fall of Mussolini, Italy surrenders

Year	Arts & Science	History & Politics
1944	T. S. Eliot's *Four Quartets*	Leningrad relieved; Allies capture Rome and land in Normandy; de Gaulle enters Paris; V1 and V2 rocket raids on London
1945	Orwell's *Animal Farm*; Nobel Prize for medicine to Alexander Fleming, E. B. Chain and Howard Florey, for discovery of penicillin	Yalta Conference; Russians capture Warsaw and Berlin; Mussolini executed, Hitler's suicide; United Nations Charter; end of the Second World War in Europe; death of President Roosevelt; atomic bombs dropped on Hiroshima and Nagasaki; Japan surrenders; Labour win General Election; Attlee Prime Minister
1946	Electronic Brain constructed at Pennsylvania University; Cocteau's film *La Belle et La Bête*; Eugene O'Neill's *The Iceman Cometh*	First General Assembly of the United Nations; nationalization of Civil Aviation, coal and the Bank of England; Churchill's 'Iron Curtain' speech
1947	Transistor invented	GATT established
1948	Norman Mailer's *The Naked and the Dead*	National Health Service; Israel founded; East German blockade of Berlin; Allied airlift into Berlin
1949	Orwell's *1984*	West Germany established, confirming division of Europe
1950	Death of Orwell	Start of Korean War

INTRODUCTION

'Evolution is the form of all life in time, man and his acts included.'
H. G. Wells, G. P. Wells and Julian Huxley, *The Science of Life*[1]

'Suppose the monkey drives the machine, the gullible, mischievous, riotous and irresponsible monkey?' V. S. Pritchett, *The Living Novel*[2]

*

I have few, vivid memories of my grandfather. A very old man of few words, and, it seemed, few pleasures. He spent most of his time in his armchair, in which no-one else dared sit, buried behind his newspaper, reviewing a world of which, I now suspect, he knew little. His life ran almost from the American Civil War to Suez – from the horse and cart to the space rocket. He was probably ill-at-ease with the twentieth century, and was, as I soon learnt, a Victorian – a man whose values had been formed in the middle of the old Queen's reign and matured well before her death. He was also the same age as Herbert George Wells of Bromley, Kent. Wells was a man very much of our century, very much it might be said a man of the next century – but he too began his life as eminently Victorian. The past is closer than you think.

*

The term 'Victorian' is used too loosely to encompass a sequence of eras, the diverse reign of a woman who lent her name to objects as diverse as a railway terminus and a plum. Too often it is used interchangeably with Dickensian – ignoring the fact that Dickens, like most novelists, set his work largely in the period of his youth and childhood, which is pre-Victorian. The era into which H. G. Wells was born was not, by any calculation, even the last Victorian era. To split a hair, it could be called late middle – much like the mid-Victorian world, an age of industry, but not yet the age of empire that was the largest part of the Queen's long widowhood – it was a god-fearing, complacent age, an age of steam and iron and crinoline. And to layer the past and its proximity even more – as Wells's autobiography states so clearly – it was a time in the nineteenth century when the influence of the eighteenth could still be felt – Wells saw it in his parents and his teachers – a generation born in the teens and twenties of the century.

Britain in the year of Wells's birth, was a qualified democracy. His mother did not have the vote – no British woman did until 1918 – and his father would almost certainly have failed to qualify under the property requirements. There had been no extension of the franchise since 1832 – a second Reform Bill failed in 1866, the year of Wells's birth, but was passed the following year at which point Joseph Wells, then aged forty, most probably gained the right to vote.

England was approaching civilization in that the citizen could no longer be hanged for stealing a loaf of bread, but if convicted of one of the remaining capital offences he/she could still be hanged in public until 1868 – and as recently as five years before Wells's birth convicts were still transported to Tasmania. Less than ten years before Wells's birth the Russian novelist Tolstoy witnessed a public guillotining in Paris – none of his major novels were yet written, and the brutality of the era strongly influenced the morality and course of those future novels. Dickens was still writing and speaking – Tolstoy came to hear him in 1861 – but his best work was behind him. George Eliot was a 'beginner' with *Adam Bede* and *The Mill on the Floss* already published and her greatest work ahead. Thomas Hardy had not yet published his first novel.

Madame Bovary was less than ten years old, as were Paddington Station and *The Guardian* newspaper. The newspaper, and magazines such as those run by Dickens, were state-of-the-art media, in this highly un-mediated world – much as the steam engine was state-of-the-art transport, in a world so slow moving that most people would probably travel no more than twenty-five miles from their home in a lifetime. Still in the Victorian future were radio, the underground railway, the electric light, the moving picture, the internal combustion engine, the telephone, those engines of mediation that make the highly-mediated world in which we have lived ever since – the 'paraphernalia of our new environment' that

Wells 'installed ... in our imagination'.[3] And while both Wells and Verne could send men to the moon in their fiction before the end of the century, powered flight was a dream not far short of fantasy – so much so that even Wells failed to predict quite how soon into the next century it would actually be achieved.[4]

*

Wells grew up in a house lit by gas – not even, he says, gas filaments, but naked gas jets (no private house had electricity until 1882). It had an outside lavatory (common enough even in the mid-twentieth century), right next to the well which was the source of all water for the entire household, and a major health hazard. The family was unusually small for the times. Three sons and one daughter – the girl died young of the then incurable appendicitis – were born to Sarah and Joseph Wells, shopkeepers in 'a nation of shopkeepers'.

When Wells was five the 1871 Education Act extended public education to the children of the lower classes with the founding of National Schools, but, as Wells put it, along strictly lower class lines to fit such children for their lower class life to come. Sarah Wells paid, instead, for Bert's attendance at Mr Morley's Commercial Academy. Compulsory schooling was introduced in 1880 and finally became free in 1891, by which time Wells was himself a teacher. The educational reform that took place, whilst it did not immediately benefit Wells's secondary education, did create the system and the opportunity for him to study for a degree at the Normal School of Science (NSS) in London's Kensington, on a scholarship. Wells attributes the lucky break as much to his broken leg in adolescence as to reform. Laid up for weeks, he became an avaricious reader. Like so many novelists, he was, essentially, self-taught. The results of his reading, the NSS and his native intelligence, freed him from what might otherwise have been a life in drapering, and turned loose upon the world of English Letters a maverick intellect – a high-tech mind in a low-tech world.

*

The recent Victorian past was changing faster than anyone could absorb. Faster, as Wells so often put it, than most people could notice. Hence the pervading late-Victorian illusion of stasis – and nothing shook that society more than debate over Charles Darwin's theory of Evolution, the greatest scientific rumpus since the trial of Galileo.

At the NSS Wells read for a general Science degree, as a trainee teacher. The first year was given over to the study of Biology, an actively controversial subject, taught by one of the most prominent thinkers of the time, Thomas Henry Huxley, zoologist and geologist, and the originator of the terrifying term 'Agnostic'.

Whilst still a schoolboy and apprentice draper, Wells had discovered the work of both Herbert Spencer, that long-forgotten social thinker and popularizer of Darwin, and T. H. Huxley. When studying with an Anglican priest for confirmation into the Church – a necessity of the job of a pupil-teacher – he took the opportunity to cross-examine the priest on the subject of Evolution. As he said himself, he was 'born blaspheming' and believed in the fire and brimstone God of his mother only as long as it took him to shake it off.

Britain in the mid-nineteenth century had 40,000 or more churches and chapels – roughly one for every six hundred people. Many of its public institutions, in particular its universities, were dominated by churchmen. In the early seventeenth century Archbishop Ussher, of Armagh, had set the date of the Creation as 4004 BC on Sunday 23 October. It would be fatuous to suggest that most English people believed this as precisely as Ussher uttered it by the 1850s. Nonetheless Wells is adamant that . . .

> Until a century ago and less,[5] the whole Christianized world felt bound to believe, and did believe, that the universe had been specially created in the course of six days by the word of God a few thousand years before . . .

Wells captured the sense of certainty in the culture of his youth, the age of progress and, with remarkable skill, made that sense of certainty dissolve in a swift descent from the God he was abolishing down to his own place in that pre-ordained order. The sense of freedom in realizing that it was not pre-ordained, although people would still speak of their 'station in life' for another fifty years, is overwhelming. Science, Religion and Liberty connect as he remembers himself at fifteen in 1881:

> The stuff accumulated by the discursive reading of my earlier years, fell rapidly into place in the wider clearer vision of my

universe that was coming into being before my eyes. Science in those days insisted, if anything, overmuch upon the reign of law. The march of progress was still being made with absolute assurance, and my emancipation was unqualified. It must be hard for intelligent people nowadays to realize all that a shabby boy of fifteen could feel as the last rack of a peevish son-crucifying Deity dissolved away into blue sky, and as the implacable social barriers, as they had seemed, set to keep him in that path unto which it had pleased god to call him, weakened down to temporary fences he could see over and presently hope to climb over or push aside.[6]

When Darwin published *The Origin of Species*[7] in 1859, the idea of Evolution was far from new. Indeed Darwin had pondered the matter for nearly thirty years. The term itself was at least two hundred years old, and its modern meaning, of the transmutation of life forms over generations, stems from Sir Charles Lyell's *Principles of Geology* published in 1832. In 1852 Herbert Spencer laid out a general Theory of Evolution, and the following year, translating Comte, Harriet Martineau first used the phrase 'Social Evolution'. The roots of the idea can be found in Bonnet's ideas of 'pre-formation' in 1762, and Darwin scrupulously lists his intellectual antecedents in the introduction to the sixth edition of *The Origin*.

The first edition sold out a print run of 1250 on day one. This statistic should not be surprising. It was the age of the gentleman-amateur naturalist and works of Natural History outsold fiction in the mid-nineteenth century.

What Darwin offered for the first time was proof,[8] with the idea of Natural Selection, of the descent of species, man included. His hesitation in publishing reflects the magnitude of his discovery – 'it is like confessing a murder'.[9] Only when his colleague Alfred Russell Wallace arrived at the same proof and prepared to publish did Darwin finally present the findings that had become evident to him on the voyage of HMS Beagle in the 1830s. The comparison to Galileo is not meant lightly. Galileo removed the earth from the centre of God's Universe, and with that offered the possibility that humanity was not at the centre of Creation and hence not its central object or purpose. Darwin abolished the Garden of Eden, the Fall of Man and Original Sin in one fell swoop. The resistance was bound to be tough. Darwin, mild, respectable and reclusive, who had once considered entering the church as a young man, was dubbed 'the most dangerous man in England'. But advocacy fell to a man who found debate and controversy irresistible, the *real* most dangerous man in England, Thomas Henry Huxley, nicknamed 'Darwin's Bulldog'.[10]

Wells summed up the impact of Huxley in an essay written for *The Listener* in 1935. It is a striking piece, indicative of the permanence of Huxley's influence and of the way opposition to Huxley became for Wells the paradigm of sloppy scientific thought and political fraud:

> I was Huxley's disciple in 1885, and I am proud to call myself his disciple in 1935. I wish I had followed his example of cool-headed deliberate thinking, plain statement and perfect sincerity more completely. But few of us have the steadfastness of his mental quality. Clear thought is the quintessence of human life. In the end its acid power will disintegrate all the force and flummery of current passions and pretences, eat the life out of every false loyalty and out of every craven creed, and bite its way through to a world of light and truth. That faith was confirmed in me by Huxley, and I have held to it for half a century because he lived and I knew him.[11]

Darwin did not invent the phrase 'survival of the fittest' – that was Herbert Spencer – and his adoption of the phrase might merely be bowing to the inevitable. Even so it might more accurately be stated as survival of those 'most fitted', in the sense of 'suited' or 'adapted'. Instead it came quickly to be interpreted, and still is, as 'strongest', and inadvertently the phrase lent weight to notions of 'might is right', 'the weak go to the wall', the colossal Imperial arrogance of late-Victorian Britain, and further afield such nonsense as Nietzschean Übermensch and Nazi Master-Race. Even as it was rejected and resisted it worked its way into the ethos. Darwin even said that his use of the phrase 'struggle for existence' was a metaphor. More often it is taken literally, and it is a literal meaning that Wells gives to it in *The Time Machine*. The plot of *The Time Machine* is the plot of Evolution[12] – and, as becomes slowly clear, Evolution runs backwards.[13]

Man gets smaller, machinery gets bigger – a not unreasonable assumption, even if it is the opposite of what has happened in just the first hundred years since *The Time Machine*. The species divides and, with division, degenerates. The Morlocks are single-diet single-environment creatures, as over-adapted as giant tortoises. The diversity of human adaptation – our ability to live anywhere and eat practically anything – has ended. The Eloi are physically and mentally weak – the surrender of the struggle for existence has caused most faculties and abilities to atrophy. This is Darwinism at its purest. As the Traveller's hypotheses get more accurate, the logic becomes more Darwinian. The Eloi's dumb beauty is far from the cerebral, almost discorporeal ugliness of the super-intelligent future-man Wells thought up at the NSS as *The Man Of The Year Million*. And after degeneration? There is a boldness in the way Wells pushes on beyond man, a biological assumption without biological arrogance, to a world where the most advanced life-form appears to be a species of giant crab, to a world beyond the beyond – we are lichen, one of the most primitive forms of life – we are slime, waiting to become planetary soup once more. And after that we will be stardust.[14]

In 1895 Wells was on the brink of success. He had pursued science in the eight years since leaving the NSS, as teacher, journalist, short-story writer and now novelist. He sent a copy of *The Time Machine* to his old teacher Huxley. The gesture was just in time as Huxley died later the same year. Wells never exaggerated his relationship with Huxley. He had attended his lectures for only one of his three years at the NSS, and there had been no personal contact with him, although this in no way diminishes the influence Huxley had on the young Wells. Darwin had always been extremely cautious on the subject of God, not doubting the truth of his own work, but well aware of the dilemma it caused for the faith of his youth. Huxley had found the term 'Agnostic' expedient, even if his defence of the term is bullish, and on the matter of God he too could show tact: '. . . the problem of the ultimate cause of existence is one which seems to me to be helplessly out of reach of my poor powers.'[15] Yet, such measured words notwithstanding, many writers have considered the influence of Huxley on Wells as pessimism – the harsh, scientific realism, that Wells absorbed reading and listening to Huxley. The idea in *The Time Machine*, of reversing evolution, is contained in Huxley's lecture of 1892, *Evolution and Ethics*, in which he coined the term 'retrogressive metamorphosis' stating that 'all forms of life will die out'.

The Time Machine is one step beyond Darwin, one step beyond

Huxley, in its extrapolation of *the* Victorian idea, Evolution. In its heady pursuit of the extinction of man, it is godless.[16]

*

The same year also saw the publication of two other definitively Victorian works, one of which was Isabella Beetons' *Book of Household Management*.[17] Far more than a cookery book, it is a model of how to run that microcosm of the state, the Victorian, quasi-geologically-layered house, with the respectable God-fearing family literally at its centre, and the servants, sleeping in the attic, and working in the cellar. The other, Samuel Smiles's *Self-Help*, offered self-improvement for the working man, a gospel of thrift, a doctrine of the individual, a well-meaning example of the convolutions of virtue under capitalism, a handbook for being a bit fitter in the struggle of the survival of the fittest.

The proximity of these three texts is far from co-incidental. It is the flip side of the coin – as Darwin pulls the rug from beneath Victorian society, its solid respectability, its sense of order and its self-regarding virtue assert themselves, again. Consider the opening of *The Time Machine* and compare its tone and effect to the opening of Conrad's Marlow stories, where a yacht is usually to be found anchored in the Thames as the glow of summer sunset prefaces a captivating yarn of moral and physical peril – 'in the destructive element immerse'.[18]

Looking back from the thirties to the last drafts of *The Time Machine*, Wells wrote:

> I had realized that the more impossible the story I had to tell, the more ordinary must be the setting, and the circumstances in which I now set the Time Traveller were all that I could imagine of solid upper-class comforts.[19]

The opening paragraph is lush with the post-prandial comfort of a good Victorian dining-room. The scene establishes the Traveller, with his taste for jokes, and his audience, one of whom is the narrator of the outer tale, as eminently respectable. It is to an audience very like this one – Doctor, Newspaper Editor, Provincial Mayor, Psychologist *et al* – that the Traveller tells the eventual tale of his exploration of the year 802,701. The narration within narration becomes an important element in the plausibility of the tale. We see what the Traveller sees, but we also see the resistances of the incredulous, Victorian audience, safe in the dining-room, via the first person, even as he acknowledges their incredulity by telling them that he 'cannot expect you to believe it' and by doing so appealing over their heads to ours. Indeed, many chapters and perils pass before it dawns on the modern reader that he has travelled into the future dressed, not like Indiana Jones, but in a tail-coat.

The society that is his audience is about to be destroyed. Wells depicts no other between[21] the Victorian present, and the year of the Eloi and Morlocks. It is, in effect, the Victorian Future. The society we see at ease among the chenille and velvet of a Richmond villa is the logical, the direct, ancestor of the one we find in 802,701.

The Traveller's exploration of that world is given as a series of hypotheses, or educated-but-wrong guesses. The first hint of expectation occurs in the opening chapter. Wells entertains, and ultimately avoids the issue of paradox, but as the diners air the possibilities and paradoxes of time travel, the Very Young Man says: 'One might invest one's money, leave it to accumulate interest, and hurry on ahead!' Such innocence might indicate an age which knew little of inflation, but the reply of the narrator is more pointed: 'To discover a society, erected on a strictly communistic basis.'

So many of the hypotheses that the Traveller tumbles forth about the society of the Eloi rest on this idea, that some sort of communistic, socialist, utopian change has come about, that the explanation of what he sees lies not in continuity but in radical change. Wells belonged to organizations advocating radical change, and when he didn't belong he did not cease to be socialist or utopian, he did not cease to argue for change or to warn against the present course. But then, the warning is aimed at the very people working for change.

In his memoirs Wells remembered his introduction to Socialism – the heady days sitting . . .

> in that little out-house at Hammersmith, a raw student again, listening to a lean, young Shaw . . .'
> . . . (the Socialist movement's) various forms were all responsive adaptations disguised even in the projectors's minds, as heroically revolutionary innovations.

... We denounced individualism; we denounced *laissez-faire*. The ownership of the land and industrial capital was to be 'vested in the community'. We did not say what we meant by the 'community' because none of us knew – or had even thought it might require knowing. But what we saw as in a vision was a world without a scramble for possession and without the motive of proprietary advantage crippling and vitiating every creative and intellectual effort. A great light had shone upon us and we could see no more ... There had been a conspicuous absence from about the cradle-side of Socialism, of men with the scientific habit of mind ... nobody sighed and said 'And *now* what?' Nobody said 'Here is a great and inspiring principle which does in general terms meet the stresses of our time, let us go on at once to test it soundly and work out its necessary particulars and methods.' Instead Socialism was proclaimed as a completed panacea.[22]

This is picked up by Sir Victor Pritchett, in terms that echo *The Time Machine* and the theory of Evolution, and he uses it to point out the innovation in Wells's writing:

It is exciting and emancipating to believe we are one of nature's latest experiments, but what if the experiment is unsuccessful? What if it is unsurmountably unpleasant? Suppose the monkey drives the machine, the gullible, mischievous, riotous and irresponsible monkey? It is an interesting fact that none of Wells's optimistic contemporaries considered such a possibility.[23]

Throughout his life Wells veered between optimism and pessimism – between the hopeful socialist and the sceptical evolutionist – not manic depression, but more a matter of intellectual phases, some of which could last for years. He was optimistic in the wake of the First World War,[24] which he had called 'the war to end wars' and he held his spirits up for the first few years of Hitler's reign of terror, but by the late thirties his optimism had waned. Towards the end of his life, in the midst of the war *after* 'the war to end wars', he seemed to go into a terminal pessimism – into an irredeemable disappointment with his ideals and with the era he had helped bring into being. Often, as in *The Time Machine*, the one fought the other, optimism versus pessimism, biology versus socialism, almost, it would seem, entropy[25] versus hope, and there is in the unravelling of humanity, the devolution that is the course of the novel, a constant frustration of the political dreams of the eighties and nineties. The Traveller himself is representative of nineties man, and the wrong guesses he makes are the perceptions of a man steeped in the Utopias of the *fin de siècle*.

The Traveller's first reaction to the future is a presumption of progress, that he himself might appear primitive, allied to a gut-reaction expressed as 'What if cruelty had grown into a common passion?' But the first sight of the Eloi leaves little room for doubt or fear – a purple tunic, sandals, curly hair, mild eyes, elfin beauty, vegetarianism, nothing much to do but eat and sleep – surely he has landed in a pseudo-greek utopia?

> 'Communism,' said I to myself.

And there follows the first of a dozen wrong-headed lectures on society – on the subject of sex and child-rearing along what he presumes to be Platonic lines – leading to the Edenic . . .

> the whole earth had become a garden.

And to an unmistakable statement of a late-Victorian Socialist ideal . . .

> Some day all of this will be better organized and still better. That is the drift of the current in spite of the eddies. The whole world will be intelligent, educated, and cooperating . . .

The literature of the end of the century is littered with utopias – in America alone there were more than a hundred in the last fifteen years, mostly inspired by Edward Bellamy's *Looking Backward* (1887). The influence of Bellamy's novel shows in Wells's work and particularly in *When the Sleeper Wakes* (1899). Bellamy re-ordered industrial life in his future-world in the interests of harmony and created a utopia. Wells re-ordered it in the interest of order *per se* and created a nightmare.

The model for *The Time Machine* is less Bellamy than William Morris.[26] Morris's *News from Nowhere* (1890) features a man who wakes after a long sleep to find himself in the twenty-first century, in a rural, rational, communistic Britain, of skilled craftsmen and youthful, beautiful people. Several novels of the time offered something like this – Richard Jefferies's *After London* (1885) and W. H. Hudson's *A Crystal Age* (1887). Wells took the prevalent late-Victorian rural paradise and overturned it – *The Time Machine* is *Bad News from Nowhere*.

Several times, while still formulating his theory of the Eloi and the future utopia, the Traveller catches glimpses of the other surviving life-form. The Morlocks are seen as 'some white animal ... in the dim light, I took for a small deer' or 'mere creatures of the half-light'. At the same time he is guessing at the purpose of the cupolas and what appear to be wells, remarking, with perhaps an unconscious pun, on 'the oddness of wells still existing'. It is a slow revelation littered with clues: the sly, gruesome reference to the Eloi as 'delicious'; the clear reference to reverse evolution in 'people unfamiliar with speculations such as those of the younger Darwin, forget that the planets must ultimately fall back one by one into the parent body'; the sightings that lead him to see the Morlocks as anthropoid, 'forearms held very low', or as a 'Lemur'; and the observation on the size of their eyes prompting comparison to a cat or an owl, without the logical conclusion that this might indicate a carnivore. Even before he descends into the under-world the Traveller has enough to reformulate his theory of the future, and with that reformulation the utopia at last dissolves and Wells thrusts the issue back at the nineteenth century as *Bad News*, where its social institutions and divisions have taken biological form, and, as much as anything is permanent, biological permanence.

> Even now, does not an East End worker live in such artificial conditions as to be practically cut off from the natural surface of the earth?

The new theory is as partial as any of his others, but after this it is impossible for the Traveller to think in utopian terms and the rest of the book is, however vaguely and speculatively, a matter of degeneration. The old century is now prominent in the working model of the new. Its ills and vices are carried over.

The origin of this sunless world inhabited by the lower classes is easily found in Wells's own life. As an infant he spent much of his waking life in the basement of his parents' shop in Bromley. Towards the top of the wall was a grating and a window, through which the young Wells could glimpse the outside world, almost entirely in terms of passing feet. Years later he titled an address to the Fabian society 'This Misery of Boots', an apt metaphor for the deprivation he had known, and which the many who had not emerged into the light still endured. The experience was reinforced by life at Uppark, the mansion near Chichester, to which his mother went as house-keeper, and in which the servants moved unseen by the masters through a labyrinth of underground tunnels.[27] It cannot be surprising that Wells came to see the underworld as the almost-natural element of the lower classes or that he should eventually project that underworld into the life of the monstrously adapted Morlocks.[28] What is surprising are the twists and turns Wells gives to it – the way he invokes and withdraws our sympathies as nineteenth-century man moves between the two societies, now irrevocably cast as two life forms, and the way he slowly releases the surprise that the result of years of oppression is dominance. The relationship between master and man has, bizarrely, reversed itself. And the worst of the Bad News is the ultimate transgression – cannibalism – and however Wells qualifies it, it is ultimately alienating.

(Man's) prejudice against human flesh is no deep-seated instinct. And so these inhuman sons of men – ! (Ch. 7)

Many critics have remarked on the violence of the Traveller. He has contempt for the cultural and generic surrender of the Eloi, but his violence towards the Morlocks is, inescapably, nasty. Once the position of the Eloi as victims has been revealed, and their child-like frailty repeatedly emphasized through the Traveller's relationship with Weena, the reader is again subject to the trickery of a Wellsian reversal. Our sympathies, however cloyed by the silliness of Weena, lie with the Eloi, the descendants of the Victorian oppressor. Only after the worst of the Traveller's violence do we overcome the revulsion of cannibal-ism enough to respond sympathetically to the descendants of the common man.

Upon the hillside were some thirty or forty Morlocks, dazzled by the light and heat, and blundering hither and thither against each other in their bewilderment. At first I did not realize their blindness, and struck furiously at them with my bar, in a frenzy of fear, as they approached me, killing one and crippling several more. But when I had watched the gestures of one of them groping under the hawthorn against the red sky, and heard their moans, I was assured of their absolute helplessness and misery in the glare, and I struck no more at them. (Ch. 9)

When the critic Samuel Hynes writes that 'the best represen-
tation of [the lower classes] is not ... realistic: it is Wells's
description of the Morlocks, the evolved underworld creatures
of *The Time Machine*', it is a startling tribute to Wells, and a
stinging criticism of the failure of realistic fiction at the turn of
the century to convey class as an issue.[29]

Chapter Eight, called 'The Palace of Green Porcelain' in the
first edition, is an all-out assault on culture. The Traveller and
Weena explore a vast ruin that holds the last vestiges of human
art and science – the skull of a Megatherium, the ribs of a
Brontosaurus, a crumbling library, the dust of a million books,
glass exhibit cases still sealed and as airtight as the day they
were closed. This ruin is the South Kensington of Wells's youth
– the educational heart of London – by metaphor, rather than
by location, name and structure. It is his own education, his
own values and the values of his teachers and fellow-socialists
that he has here reduced to dust and rubble – they have
'deliquesced', as he puts it.

> Here and there I found traces of the little people in the shape of
> rare fossils broken to pieces or threaded in strings upon reeds.
> (Ch. 8)

I doubt that any 'child' of T. H. Huxley's would have written
such a sentence blithely. The gaps in the fossil record were huge,
the opposition to Darwin and Huxley would exploit the holes
in the evidence in the effort to demolish the theory. Precious
fossils threaded into necklaces is contrivedly primitivist, invok-
ing notions of savagery, and in a single image striking at the
heart of the intellectual life of the age. And there follows a scene
which is surely designed to shock his contemporaries, as Wells
has Weena and the Traveller dance in – and on – the grave of
Nineties culture.[30]

> And so, in that derelict museum, upon the thick soft carpeting of
> dust, to Weena's huge delight, I solemnly performed a kind of
> composite dance, whistling *The Land of the Leal*, as cheerfully as
> I could. It was in part a modest *can-can*, in part a step-dance, in
> part a skirt-dance (so far as my tail-coat permitted), and in part
> original. For I am naturally inventive, as you know.

The word 'solemnly' should not mislead. (How, in or out of a
tail-coat, does one *solemnly* dance a can-can, or a step-dance,

which, after all, must be pretty much a Dixieland cake-walk?)
What follows is qualified by the 'naturally inventive' more than
the 'solemnly' and, it is, I would argue, in the socialist, literary
world of the 1890s – the world of Shaw and Morris – well-nigh
outrageous.

So much that mattered, so much that was held to be the key
to the grasping of future – books, science, education – lies in
ruins. Their existence has done nothing to halt the degeneration
of the species. Reading the novel is a process of detection, as
Wells mercilessly pits the logic of devolution against the ideals
of Socialism, we share with the Traveller the slow, systematic
revelations that demolish the optimistic, utopian beliefs of that
'out-house in Hammersmith',[31] of the Science School's Debating
Society, of left-wing intellectual London.

*

On occasion Wells has been portrayed as a purveyor of pseudo-
science.[32] Lately, several critics have taken the opposite tack and
pointed to Wells's legitimate qualifications in science, and in
particular the logical, scientific method in which an initially
improbable notion is pursued.[33] Whilst subsequent science fiction has been pre-occupied with the mechanics of time travel,
and with the paradox of it,[34] Wells avoids both the mechanics
and the paradox in *The Time Machine*.[35] The novel seems to be
an exception to the logically pursued preposterous idea that is
the basis of *The New Accelerator* or *The First Men in the Moon*.
Until, that is, one substitutes the process of evolution for the
process of time travel and allows that the latter theme serves the
former. Wells cut from the final version any time travel
backwards, which would inescapably have pushed the temporal
paradox to the foreground. The origin of the story in the idea of
Four-Dimensional geometry, the 'Universe Rigid', as Wells calls it,
he recorded several times, and a short debate on the matter serves
as introduction to the novel – indeed the New Review version
contained the phrase 'a Rigid Universe' – but thereafter the matter
does not concern Wells. The possibility in the act of time travel
becomes remarkably singular, once reduced to forward motion.
As he put it in the 1931 Preface to the Random House edition:

The only difference between the time dimension and the others
... lay in the movement of consciousness along it, whereby the
progress of the present was constituted.

Wells then adds that before Einstein the vocabulary to cope with
this did not exist and ... 'So my opening exposition escapes
along the line of paradox to an imaginative romance.' Wells
thought the book uneven because of this, saying that it opened
much better than it closed. He gives up on the temporal paradox
and doesn't much bother with the machine, offering the merest
teases of description and avoiding the detail that would strain
plausibility, but *The Time Machine* does not become just a yarn.
It is a hard-nosed political fable for his time, with Evolution as
its outward appearance. And it is a warning.

In the *Pall Mall Gazette*, in 1895, Wells set forth the warning
in far blunter terms. In a tacky piece of journalism, he wrote, in
italics:

> ... *in no case does the record of the fossils show a really dominant
> species succeeded by its own descendants.*

The peak of a species' ascendancy is the eve of its overthrow.
He then reiterates the idea of the crab as the future, pointing out
that fossils suggest there were once six-foot long land crabs
(which ought to imply, in his terms, that they had had their day,
unless Evolution run backwards is the *precise* reverse of Evolution run forwards) moving on to ants and octopuses as the shape
of things to come. He envisages giant octopuses strolling eight-
legged up the beaches to pick off ...

> the excursionists ... soon it would become a common feature of
> the watering places ... Even now, for all we can tell, the coming
> terror may be crouching for its spring and the fall of humanity be
> at hand.[36]

This is pot-boiling stuff, and I suspect it was written as publicity
for *The Time Machine*. The warning in *The Time Machine* is
double-edged – it warns of the perils of the divisive English class
system, and it warns of the biological arrogance of our species.
However badly expressed, it was a theme that Wells cared
deeply about, and, odd bouts of optimism excepted, it was one
he stood by. In 1942 he seemed to hark back directly to *The
Time Machine* in *The Conquest of Time*:

I am convinced that the species we so prematurely call Homo Sapiens is bound to extinguish itself unless is now sets about adapting itself at a great rate to the stresses it has brought down upon itself. But if it does that it will become a new species of self-conscious animal. It seems improbable, though it is not impossible, that it will cease to interbreed freely, and so long as it does not do that it will not split into two or more divergent species; it will evolve *en bloc*.[37]

*

In the 1931 Preface, Wells wrote an account of the ideas in the book, which is oddly optimistic, almost revisionist, startlingly modest, and soon eclipsed:

It seems a very undergraduate performance now ... But it goes as far as his philosophy about human evolution went in those days ... the geologists and astronomers of that time told us dreadful lies about the 'inevitable' freezing up of the world – and of life and mankind with it. The whole game of life would be over in a million years or less ...

This is backtracking. Wells even adds that the extension of probable age of the earth means ...

that man will be able to go anywhere and do anything[38]

Wells was too often dismissive of his early work in an effort to shift attention to what he was writing in the twenties and thirties. The dismissal should deceive no-one. Like it or not, the early work (Kipps, Mr Polly et al, as well as the Scientific Romances) remains the achievement for which he is remembered, and even then his rejection of old forms was hardly ever a rejection of old ideas. Thirteen years later, in 1944, the fundamental idea behind *The Time Machine* was forcefully reasserted, quite possibly for the last time, in a book published two years before Wells's death. Once again he comes back to the abiding figure of his fiction – the hero-scientist,[39] and once again he comes back to the values the bleak future of *The Time Machine* had demolished, as another society destroys itself around him:

We are learning biological modesty very reluctantly. We make Man the measure of our universe, and the same sort of self-satisfaction that dubbed our sort *Homo Sapiens*, and his biological kindred Primates, blinds us to the many alternative cards our hard and vindictive mother Nature may have up her sleeve for us, if we prove too recalcitrant offspring. Numerous insectivores and rodent types may be acquiring characteristics with survival value. There may even be insects, ants for example, acquiring qualities that will oust and exterminate us. Forms may be arising whose weapon will be mortal human epidemics to which they are immune ... Only the hard-thinking man with the microscope, working without haste and without delay, can hope to anticipate and avert that attack upon mankind. The acquisitive fool with his money bags, the priest with his prayers and incantations, the straining girl in the factory, even the gallant lad in the stokehold of the labouring ship or behind the tommy gun, can do nothing against our ultimate supreme enemy, Ignorance. Knowledge or extinction. There is no other choice for man.[40]

JOHN LAWTON

References

1. Cassell 1931, p. 193.
2. V. S. Pritchett, *The Living Novel*, Chatto & Windus 1946, p. 122.
3. *Ibid.*, p. 123
4. In *Anticipations*, 1901. Wells offers no date sooner than 1950.
5. Wells wrote this circa 1919. *The Outline of History*, Cassell 1951, p. 976.
6. H. G. W., *Experiment in Autobiography*, Faber & Faber 1984, p. 144 (first pub. 1934).
7. *The Origin of Species by Means of Natural Selection* or *The Preservation of Favoured Species in the Struggle for Life*, John Murray 1859.
8. The fossil record being very inadequate at this time and the work of Gregor Mendel on Heredity, whilst published in 1865, being virtually ignored for forty years (the modern term Genetics dates only from 1905), 'proof' was subject to debate and contradiction for the rest of Darwin's life and beyond.
9. Letter to Joseph Hooker, 1844, quoted in J. W. Burrow's introduction to *The Origin of Species*, Penguin 1982, p. 32; and in William Irvine's *Apes, Angels & Victorians*, Weidenfeld & Nicolson 1955, p. 72.

10. If this biblical row, and Wells's passionate attack on the enemies of truth, seem so long ago as to be diminished in importance or impossible 'to see what the fuss was about' – let me bring the matter up to date. In 1925 a schoolteacher in Dayton, Tennessee, one John T. Scopes, was prosecuted by the State of Tennessee for teaching the theory of Evolution. Such was the interest in 'the Monkey Trial' that it was broadcast live by a Chicago radio station. Scopes lost, won on appeal in the Tennessee Supreme Court, thereby preventing the Supreme Court of the United States from reviewing the matter for all states, and in the wake three more bible-belt states passed laws on the subject. As recently as 1985 Louisiana retained a statute from that time requiring equal time to be given to the teaching in schools of the story of the Creation.

The idea that Darwin said man was descended from monkeys, untrue though it is, was quickly, and permanently taken up by his opponents. The most famous example occurred when Bishop Wilberforce asked T. H. Huxley, in a debate in 1860, on which side, his mother's or his father's, was he descended from a monkey? Huxley's reply, though less jokey, was withering. In a curious way the persistence of the idea registers in the quotation from Pritchett with which this introduction opens. Huxley's 'Man's Place in Nature', published in 1863, before Darwin's 'The Descent of Man', was greeted by Thomas Carlyle as 'the monkey damnification of mankind'.

11. H. G. Wells, *Thomas Henry Huxley, The Listener*, 9 October 1935, p. 595.

12. In *The Penguin Companion to Literature*, vol. 1, 1971, Angus Ross sums up the impact of the theory of Evolution thus: 'the theory had great influence on the writing of fiction. It strengthened the tendency to naturalistic description, the notion of "character", and the tendency to length, to give material and scope to show change at work' p. 134. Which is surely accurate if applied to mainstream novels, but says nothing about *The Time Machine* or science fiction as a whole.

13. What power analogy? What does one medium learn from another? The moving picture was brand new in 1895 and whilst I can find no report that Wells went to the 'Kinema', would the plot of running evolution backwards be so accessible without the possibilities made visible in film? Would the last glimpses of Mrs Watchett skimming backwards across the room have been written

without it? Wells was, also, almost certainly, the first novelist to be asked about the film rights in his book. Robert W. Paul, inventor of cinematic projection, approached Wells at the end of 1895.

14. The Appendix to this edition contains a long scene immediately preceding the scene with the giant crabs. It appeared in the *New Review* serialization, but not in the book edition of 1895. One reason I include it is that it makes the reversal of evolution absolutely clear – towit a marsupial stage of life has reappeared, looking distinctly as though it had once been human – although the very clarity of the scene may well be the reason Wells cut it.

15. Lecture given in 1874 to the British Association in Belfast. How tactful it was necessary to be might be discerned in the work of Sir Charles Lyell, whose *Principles of Geology* set out a theory of Evolution twenty-five years before Darwin. Lyell allows the evolution of life, but then exempts man from this – we are *created*, all other life merely *evolves*.

16. See Wells and his Critics. This disturbed the first critics who read Wells, and it is not far-fetched to say that it disturbed Sir Victor Pritchett half a century later, even if his critique rests not on the faith but the innate morality of man.

17. Mrs Beeton's text was first published in *The English Woman's Domestic Magazine*, run by Mr Beeton, in monthly parts, from 1859. The book version appeared in 1861.

18. Joseph Conrad, born in the Polish Ukraine, nine years before Wells, also published his first novel, *Almayer's Folly*, in 1895. The Marlow story 'Youth' opens in this way. 'Heart of Darkness' establishes a professional 'guest-list' much as *The Time Machine* does.

19. H. G. Wells, *Experiment in Autobiography*, Faber & Faber 1984, p. 516. (first pub. 1934).

20. For his own time, if not for ours, Wells established the credentials of the audience. In Chapter Two the narrator says that he has recently encountered the doctor at the Linnaean Society – the same body to which Darwin and Wallace first made their conclusions known in 1858.

21. The 1960s Hollywood film of *The Time Machine* is wise with hindsight and invents scenes in which the Traveller is witness to the First, Second and Third World Wars.

22. H. G. Wells, *Experiment in Autobiography*, Faber & Faber 1984, pp. 244, 250–51 and 215 (first pub. 1934).

23. V. S. Pritchett, *The Living Novel*, Chatto & Windus 1946, p. 122.

24. In saying this I am, without doubt, disagreeing with people who knew Wells, such as Orwell, part of whose obituary for Wells is printed in *Wells and his Critics*, p. 94.

25. See *Wells and His Critics*, p. 96, extract from Norman and Jeanne Mackenzie's *The Time Traveller*. Wells was familiar with the work of Lord Kelvin of Glasgow University, proponent of the Second Law of Thermodynamics, better known as the theory of Entropy, paraphrased as 'everything disperses in time' or 'Nature tends to disorder'.

26. Morris reviewed *Looking Backward* for *The Commonweal* in January 1889. He took an instant dislike to the book, pointing out that plots in which a man wakes up in some utopian future are now very common, and saying that Bellamy's imagination is limited – limited to extrapolating the professional middle-class, Boston and the machine. Hence his real objection to Bellamy's utopia is that it is the antithesis of his own – professional, urban and mechanized.

27. See *Wells and his Critics*, extract by Anthony West, for a fuller account of life at Uppark. It could also be argued that this experience was hybridised with the experience of life in Etruria, in the Potteries of the English Midlands, in which Wells was living when he first began to develop the story that eventually became *The Time Machine*. It was a part of England in which industrialization had sharpened the division of master and man, in which there existed a substantial working class – perhaps Wells's most obvious contact with the masses – and that this manifests itself in Chapter 6, when the Traveller descends to the underworld and discovers its caverns of vast machinery.

28. The origin of the name is obvious in the biblical 'Moloch'. Less obvious is the origin of the Eloi in the Hebrew text of Christ's questioning of God from the cross – 'Eloi, Eloi, lama sabachthani?' I am grateful to Philip Hamin for the latter point.

29. *The Edwardian Turn of Mind*, Oxford 1968, repr. Pimlico 1991, p. 63.

30. In *News from Nowhere*, which is part utopian novel, part satire on the London of his day, William Morris has lots of fun demolishing or abusing the buildings of the time. The House of Commons is one that survives into the year 2000 and wotnot, in which time it used as, and referred to as, the Dung Market. The change of name does not mean a change of content. A joke, and

not a bad one at that. What Wells does is far more savage. Morris, after all, carefully preserves the British Museum Reading Room, and its contents.

31. The 'outhouse' – almost needless to say – belonged to William Morris.

32. Kingsley Amis wrote of Wells: '[he] . . . is nearly always concerned only to fire off a few phrases of pseudo-scientific patter and bundle his characters away to the moon or the 83rd Century with despatch', *New Maps of Hell*, Gollancz 1961, p. 38.

33. The best exponents of this argument are David C. Smith and Rosslyn D. Haynes (see Suggestions for Further Reading, p. 104). I use the same point in the Introduction to the Everyman 1994 edition of *When the Sleeper Wakes*. 'If Wells's achievement – his thoroughness as a writer of science fiction – lay in the application of scientific method, then it was at its simplest a matter of adopting a premise on the fringe of contemporary thought, or even downright preposterous, and developing it in terms of scientific accuracy'. pp. xxxviii–xxxix.

34. The American critic Harry M. Geduld, in *The Definitive Time Machine*, lists forty-seven novels and dramas on the theme of time travel since Wells, and even then I suspect he has only scraped the surface (Bloomington 1987).

35. *The Chronic Argonauts*, *The Time Machine's* earliest version, does not – *The Time Traveller* is a victim of temporal paradox, when he kills a man in the past.

On the mechanics of time travel – In 1927 J. W. Dunne published *An Experiment with Time*, a serious study of the subject of time travel, influenced, but not engendered by *The Time Machine*. In a revised edition Dunne answered some of his critics, including Wells, who had read and commented on the book. 'Mr H. G. Wells laments that I have taken seriously something which he never intended to be treated seriously, namely, his description of 'duration as a dimension of space', and have brooded too much upon it' (Faber & Faber 1973, p. 211). He then cites the sources of his interest as being much more than the Wells novel, and in the original edition he had given over four or five pages to describing the theories of C. H. Hinton, whose paper 'What is the Fourth Dimension?' was published in 1887. Rosslyn D. Haynes, in *H. G. Wells Discoverer of the Future*, writes that Hinton was the only literary precursor of Wells in the theory of time travel, unless one counts Wilde's *The Canterville Ghost*, which she does not, but I cannot say for certain that Wells read Hinton. What matters is that Wells's reply to Dunne shows how little the mechanics of the subject mattered to his novel.

36. H. G. Wells, *The Extinction of Man*, repr. in 'Certain Personal Matters', Lawrence & Bullen 1898, pp. 172, 179.

37. H. G. Wells, *The Conquest of Time*, Watts 1942, p. 57.

38. H. G. Wells, Preface to *The Time Machine*, Random House 1931, pp. viii–ix.

39. With this idea – the scientist as hero – Huxley inevitably raises his head. I suspect he lurks in many of Wells's hero scientists – in the Traveller, in Cavor (*The First Men in the Moon*) and, perversely, in Doctor Moreau. William Irvine, writing a biography of Huxley and Darwin in 1955, summed up the heroic model: 'The warfare between evolution and orthodoxy created a splendid dramatic opportunity, and with the quick instinct of a man of action Huxley seized it. To the cleric as the benighted and prejudiced defender of a fading superstition, he opposed the scientist, the impersonal investigator who, though somewhat satanically godless and inhumanly detached, is by virtue to his dedication and discipline devoted to truth in the field of thought, to rectitude in the field of action and – because truth is power, and in its nineteenth century form rectitude is sympathy – to humanitarian progress in both fields' (*Apes, Angels & Victorians*, Weidenfeld 1955, p. 117).

It could, of course, be argued that what Wells depicts in Cavor, is the price of detachment, and in Moreau the price of inhuman detachment. I doubt that godlessness was ever satanic where Wells was concerned.

40. H. G. Wells, '*42–44; A Contemporary Memoir*', Secker & Warburg 1944, pp. 211–12.

NOTE ON THE TEXT

The Drafts of The Time Machine: A Determined Story

There were six versions of *The Time Machine* between 1888 and 1895, the date of first publication in book form. Wells began the first version whilst recuperating from kidney trouble in Etruria. It was then called *The Chronic Argonauts*, and appeared in three parts in March, April and May of 1888 in the *Science Schools Journal* – which Wells had helped to found. The germ of the idea goes back at least two years before that. In his *Autobiography* Wells states that he first heard of the idea of a Four-Dimensional geometry at the Science Schools Debating Society, and that this led him to write the paper 'The Universe Rigid', which was never published, having been turned down by Frank Harris at the *Fortnightly Review* with much damage to Wells's confidence and ego.

The *Chronic Argonauts* bears little resemblance to *The Time Machine*. The text runs to about 9000 words. The Time Traveller is named as Dr Moses Nebogipfel.[1] He is very vivid in appearance, but the narrative is extremely compressed and reads more like notes for future work than a novel or novella. The story is set in Wales, where Nebogipfel works on his time machine in a semi-ruined manse. We see none of his time travelling first hand, and the crisis of the plot occurs when the villagers storm the house accusing him of murdering a hunch-back and of being a warlock. At this point it resembles nothing quite so much as the plot of every Universal horror film, from *Frankenstein* to *Abbott and Costello meet the Wolfman*.

Over the next three years Wells produced two more versions, which have been lost for many years. Wells did, however, show them to his friend Professor A. Morley Davies, who set down his recollections for Wells's biographer Geoffrey West in 1930. The second introduces the idea of upper and lower worlds in the distant future, although man has not yet evolved into two separate species. The third dispenses with Nebogipfel and depicts a future-world ruled by an elite, who use mass hypnosis to control society.

In 1894 W. R. Henley took seven unsigned articles by Wells on the subject of time travel for the *National Observer*. 'Articles' is misleading. They read like linked stories, and were published from March to June of that year.

The date is 12,203. Nebogipfel has gone for good, and the mad scientist figure gives way to the Victorian gentleman of the 1895 novel. The structure of the future is much as it is in this final version. The Eloi are not named, but the Morlocks are. *The Time Machine* is recognizable in much of the writing: the first, third and sixth articles carry over into the final version substantially; the 'instantaneous cube' is introduced into the argument; the encounter with the Eloi is much the same, but the existence of the Morlocks is baldly stated rather than revealed through the plot; the descent into the underworld is included as is the power of matches; Weena is not yet a character, and the ending is abrupt. The future beyond the date of 12,203 is only sketched in, and an oddly human, deflationary touch, later cut, leaves the story hanging:

> He stopped abruptly. 'There is that kid of mine upstairs crying. He always cries when he wakes up in the dark. If you don't mind, I will just go up and tell him it's all right'.

The tale was unfinished when Henley left the journal. However, Henley took up a post as editor of the *New Review* in December 1894 and recommissioned Wells. Between the *National Observer* and *New Review* versions, Wells seems to have tried out many revisions of the text. Much new material was written – *The Time Machine* is well over three times the length of the *National Observer* articles and several scenes never appeared in any printed form. Manuscripts include episodes in which the Time Traveller has encounters with a prehistoric hippopotamus, with angry Puritans on 31 December 1645, and in which he dies from the effects of time travel. The story ran in the *New Review* from January to May 1895. In May *The Time Machine* finally appeared as a book, published by Heinemann, who also published the *New Review*. Mr Wells was, at long last, a published novelist.

The opening of the book, down to the words 'so I never

talked of it until – ' (p. 7), whilst covering much the same ground, is very different in expression from the opening of the *New Review* version, and Wells made a large cut from Chapter Fourteen, 'The Further Vision', (Chapter Eleven in this edition). (See Appendix.) Substantially the texts of *The Time Machine* and the *New Review* story are the same.

The Texts of The Time Machine: A Confusing Story

The history of *The Time Machine* after book publication is almost as chequered as that before.

This edition is based on the 1935 Everyman edition. That in turn was based on the *Collected Short Stories* published by Benn in 1927 (despite the title not all Wells's stories are in that volume), which in turn derives from the *Essex Collected* of 1926–7 vol. 16, and that in turn is based on the *Atlantic Collected* of 1924 vol. 1. To the best of my knowledge that is the genealogy of the present edition.

The Time Machine first appeared in book form in 1895 – published in Britain by Heinemann and in the USA by Holt. The versions differ, and the Holt edition has aroused some critical speculation. Was it put together before the *New Review* serial? Was it incomplete? The Heinemann has long been regarded as the better of the two, and it was this edition that Wells chose to revise for the *Atlantic Collected*, rearranging the sixteen titled chapters and Epilogue into twelve untitled chapters, still with Epilogue.

He had found at some point a copy of *The Time Machine* which he had marked up in 1898 or 1899 ... 'a few modifications in arrangement and improvements in expression' ... 'so what the reader gets here is a revised definitive version a quarter of a century old.'[2]

But, having pronounced it definitive, Wells then continued to make small changes, first to the *Essex Collected*, and then to the *Gollancz Collected Scientific Romances* of 1933. Again, to the best of my knowledge these latter are the last changes he made. Some diligent work was done in the late 1980s by David Lake to identify the changes.[3] He regards the Atlantic edition, whilst not error-free, as the model, so long as the later corrections are noted. I have taken his advice.

Inevitably, every time a book is reset there will be errors. And the skill of proof-reading is not getting better with the waning of the century. The Everyman edition of 1994 had accumulated many errors in the text – for which its editor was not responsible – and as far as possible I have attempted to correct them. For this edition I compared the Everyman 1994 edition to the Gollancz 1933 edition, in order to identify any textual changes made by Wells. If the two texts disagreed, or anything aroused my suspicion, I checked them against the *Atlantic* edition, and, out of nothing more than curiosity, against the 1895 Heinemann edition. Occasionally I checked the *Essex Collected*.

This text, then, follows the *Atlantic* edition in punctuation, and format, from its origin in the Everyman edition of 1935, but incorporates any textual changes Wells included in the Gollancz edition, or identified by David Lake. I do not guarantee it as perfect. I merely state that I have tried to rid it of errrors built up over the last fifty-odd years. I leave it to others to achieve the 'definitive Wells'.

I have only two points to add to what David Lake has written. He approves the Everyman 1935 edition as the 'best reprint of the Atlantic', and some American editions for their adherence to the *Atlantic* edition 'or something very like it'. I do not know which American editions he is referring to, but as far as I can tell the Everyman 1935 edition is based not directly on the Atlantic edition but on the Benn *Collected Short Stories* of 1927, as I said earlier. And the American editions I checked this year (1995) are based on the Everyman 1935 edition – or else in typesetting from the Benn edition they made exactly the same error Everyman did in 1935, as did Penguin in 1958. The second point – the error of 'patent' for 'patient' (Chapter Eight) – was introduced by the earlier Essex edition not by the Everyman 1935 edition. None of this matters much.

To add to the confusion, for Wells's 80th birthday in 1946 Penguin put the 1895 edition back into print, and in 1960 Dover, in the USA, republished the 1895 edition and included in it the long section cut from Chapter Fourteen (here, Eleven) after the last serialization. That is printed here as an appendix.

References

1. Nebo, as much as Moses, is a biblical reference. Mount Nebo occurs several times in the Old Testament, e.g. Deuteronomy 32.v.49.

2. Preface to Vol. 1 of the Atlantic *Collected Works of H. G. Wells*, 1924. p. xxii.

3. David Lake, *The Current Texts of Wells's Early Science Fiction Novels*; Situation Unsatisfactory Part 1. *The Wellsian*, Summer 1988.

THE TIME MACHINE

The Time Traveller (for so it will be convenient to speak of him) was expounding a recondite matter to us. His grey eyes shone and twinkled, and his usually pale face was flushed and animated. The fire burned brightly, and the soft radiance of the incandescent lights in the lilies of silver caught the bubbles that flashed and passed in our glasses. Our chairs, being his patents, embraced and caressed us rather than submitted to be sat upon, and there was that luxurious after-dinner atmosphere when thought runs gracefully free of the trammels of precision. And he put it to us in this way – marking the points with a lean forefinger – as we sat and lazily admired his earnestness over this new paradox (as we thought it) and his fecundity.

'You must follow me carefully. I shall have to controvert one or two ideas that are almost universally accepted. The geometry, for instance, they taught you at school is founded on a misconception.'

'Is not that rather a large thing to expect us to begin upon?' said Filby, an argumentative person with red hair.

'I do not mean to ask you to accept anything without reasonable ground for it. You will soon admit as much as I need from you. You know of course that a mathematical line, a line of thickness *nil*, has no real existence. They taught you that? Neither has a mathematical plane. These things are mere abstractions.'

'That is all right,' said the Psychologist.

'Nor, having only length, breadth, and thickness, can a cube have a real existence.'

'There I object,' said Filby. 'Of course a solid body may exist. All real things—'

'So most people think. But wait a moment. Can an *instantaneous* cube exist?'

'Don't follow you,' said Filby.

'Can a cube that does not last for any time at all, have a real existence?'

Filby became pensive. 'Clearly,' the Time Traveller proceeded, 'any real body must have extension in *four* directions: it must have Length, Breadth, Thickness, and – Duration. But through a natural infirmity of the flesh, which I will explain to you in a moment, we incline to overlook this fact. There are really four dimensions, three which we call the three planes of Space, and a fourth, Time. There is, however, a tendency to draw an unreal distinction between the former three dimensions and the latter, because it happens that our consciousness moves intermittently in one direction along the latter from the beginning to the end of our lives.'

'That,' said a very young man, making spasmodic efforts to relight his cigar over the lamp; 'that . . . very clear indeed.'

'Now, it is very remarkable that this is so extensively overlooked,' continued the Time Traveller, with a slight accession of cheerfulness. 'Really this is what is meant by the Fourth Dimension, though some people who talk about the Fourth Dimension do not know they mean it. It is only another way of looking at Time. *There is no difference between Time and any of the three dimensions of Space except that our consciousness moves along it*. But some foolish people have got hold of the wrong side of that idea. You have all heard what they have to say about this Fourth Dimension?'

'*I* have not,' said the Provincial Mayor.

'It is simply this. That Space, as our mathematicians have it, is spoken of as having three dimensions, which one may call Length, Breadth, and Thickness, and is always definable by reference to three planes, each at right angles to the others. But some philosophical people have been asking why *three* dimensions particularly – why not another direction at right angles to the other three? – and have even tried to construct a Four-Dimensional geometry. Professor Simon Newcomb was expounding this to the New York Mathematical Society only a month or so ago. You know how on a flat surface, which has only two dimensions, we can represent a figure of a three-dimensional solid, and similarly they think that by models of three dimensions they could represent one of four – if they could master the perspective of the thing. See?'

'I think so,' murmured the Provincial Mayor; and, knitting

his brows, he lapsed into an introspective state, his lips moving as one who repeats mystic words. 'Yes, I think I see it now,' he said after some time, brightening in a quite transitory manner.

'Well, I do not mind telling you I have been at work upon this geometry of Four Dimensions for some time. Some of my results are curious. For instance, here is a portrait of a man at eight years old, another at fifteen, another at seventeen, another at twenty-three, and so on. All these are evidently sections, as it were, Three-Dimensional representations of his Four-Dimensioned being, which is a fixed and unalterable thing.

'Scientific people,' proceeded the Time Traveller, after the pause required for the proper assimilation of this, 'know very well that Time is only a kind of Space. Here is a popular scientific diagram, a weather record. This line I trace with my finger shows the movement of the barometer. Yesterday it was so high, yesterday night it fell, then this morning it rose again, and so gently upward to here. Surely the mercury did not trace this line in any of the dimensions of Space generally recognized? But certainly it traced such a line, and that line, therefore, we must conclude was along the Time-Dimension.'

'But,' said the Medical Man, staring hard at a coal in the fire, 'if Time is really only a fourth dimension of Space, why is it, and why has it always been, regarded as something different? And why cannot we move in Time as we move about in the other dimensions of Space?'

The Time Traveller smiled. 'Are you so sure we can move freely in Space? Right and left we can go, backward and forward freely enough, and men always have done so. I admit we move freely in two dimensions. But how about up and down? Gravitation limits us there.'

'Not exactly,' said the Medical Man. 'There are balloons.'

'But before the balloons, save for spasmodic jumping and the inequalities of the surface, man had no freedom of vertical movement.'

'Still they could move a little up and down,' said the Medical Man.

'Easier, far easier down than up.'

'And you cannot move at all in Time, you cannot get away from the present moment.'

'My dear sir, that is just where you are wrong. That is just where the whole world has gone wrong. We are always getting away from the present moment. Our mental existences, which are immaterial and have no dimensions, are passing along the Time-Dimension with a uniform velocity from the cradle to the grave. Just as we should travel *down* if we began our existence fifty miles above the earth's surface.'

'But the great difficulty is this,' interrupted the Psychologist. 'You *can* move about in all directions of Space, but you cannot move about in Time.'

'That is the germ of my great discovery. But you are wrong to say that we cannot move about in Time. For instance, if I am recalling an incident very vividly I go back to the instant of its occurrence: I become absent-minded, as you say. I jump back for a moment. Of course we have no means of staying back for any length of time, any more than a savage or an animal has of staying six feet above the ground. But a civilized man is better off than the savage in this respect. He can go up against gravitation in a balloon, and why should he not hope that ultimately he may be able to stop or accelerate his drift along the Time-Dimension, or even turn about and travel the other way?'

'Oh, *this*,' began Filby, 'is all—'

'Why not?' said the Time Traveller.

'It's against reason,' said Filby.

'What reason?' said the Time Traveller.

'You can show black is white by argument,' said Filby, 'but you will never convince me.'

'Possibly not,' said the Time Traveller. 'But now you begin to see the object of my investigations into the geometry of Four Dimensions. Long ago I had a vague inkling of a machine—'

'To travel through Time!' exclaimed the Very Young Man.

'That shall travel indifferently in any direction of Space and Time, as the driver determines.'

Filby contented himself with laughter.

'But I have experimental verification,' said the Time Traveller.

'It would be remarkably convenient for the historian,' the Psychologist suggested. 'One might travel back and verify the accepted account of the Battle of Hastings, for instance!'

'Don't you think you would attract attention?' said the Medical Man. 'Our ancestors had no great tolerance for anachronisms.'

'One might get one's Greek from the very lips of Homer and Plato,' the Very Young Man thought.

'In which case they would certainly plough you for the Little-go. The German scholars have improved Greek so much.'

'Then there is the future,' said the Very Young Man. 'Just think! One might invest all one's money, leave it to accumulate at interest, and hurry on ahead!'

'To discover a society,' said I, 'erected on a strictly communistic basis.'

'Of all the wild extravagant theories!' began the Psychologist.

'Yes, so it seemed to me, and so I never talked of it until—'

'Experimental verification!' cried I. 'You are going to verify *that*?'

'The experiment!' cried Filby, who was getting brain-weary.

'Let's see your experiment anyhow,' said the Psychologist, 'though it's all humbug, you know.'

The Time Traveller smiled round at us. Then, still smiling faintly, and with his hands deep in his trousers pockets, he walked slowly out of the room, and we heard his slippers shuffling down the long passage to his laboratory.

The Psychologist looked at us. 'I wonder what he's got?'

'Some sleight-of-hand trick or other,' said the Medical Man, and Filby tried to tell us about a conjurer he had seen at Burslem; but before he had finished his preface the Time Traveller came back, and Filby's anecdote collapsed.

The thing the Time Traveller held in his hand was a glittering metallic framework, scarcely larger than a small clock, and very delicately made. There was ivory in it, and some transparent crystalline substance. And now I must be explicit, for this that follows – unless his explanation is to be accepted – is an absolutely unaccountable thing. He took one of the small octagonal tables that were scattered about the room, and set it in front of the fire, with two legs on the hearthrug. On this table he placed the mechanism. Then he drew up a chair, and sat down. The only other object on the table was a small shaded lamp, the bright light of which fell full upon the model. There were also perhaps a dozen candles about, two in brass candlesticks upon the mantel and several in sconces, so that the room was brilliantly illuminated. I sat in a low arm-chair nearest the fire, and I drew this forward so as to be almost between the Time Traveller and the fireplace. Filby sat behind him, looking over his shoulder. The Medical Man and the Provincial Mayor watched him in profile from the right, the Psychologist from the left. The Very Young Man stood behind the Psychologist. We were all on the alert. It appears incredible to me that any kind of trick, however subtly conceived and however adroitly done, could have been played upon us under these conditions.

The Time Traveller looked at us, and then at the mechanism. 'Well?' said the Psychologist.

'This little affair,' said the Time Traveller, resting his elbows upon the table and pressing his hands together above the apparatus, 'is only a model. It is my plan for a machine to travel through time. You will notice that it looks singularly askew, and that there is an odd twinkling appearance about this bar, as though it was in some way unreal.' He pointed to the part with his finger. 'Also, here is one little white lever, and here is another.'

The Medical Man got up out of his chair and peered into the thing. 'It's beautifully made,' he said.

'It took two years to make,' retorted the Time Traveller. Then, when we had all imitated the action of the Medical Man, he said: 'Now I want you clearly to understand that this lever, being pressed over, sends the machine gliding into the future, and this other reverses the motion. This saddle represents the seat of a time traveller. Presently I am going to press the lever, and off the machine will go. It will vanish, pass into future Time, and disappear. Have a good look at the thing. Look at the table too, and satisfy yourselves there is no trickery. I don't want to waste this model, and then be told I'm a quack.'

There was a minute's pause perhaps. The Psychologist seemed about to speak to me, but changed his mind. Then the Time Traveller put forth his finger towards the lever. 'No,' he said suddenly. 'Lend me your hand.' And turning to the Psychologist, he took that individual's hand in his own and told him to put out his forefinger. So that it was the Psychologist himself who sent forth the model Time Machine on its interminable voyage. We all saw the lever turn. I am absolutely certain there was no trickery. There was a breath of wind, and the lamp flame jumped. One of the candles on the mantel was blown out, and the little machine suddenly swung round, became indistinct, was seen as a ghost for a second perhaps, as an eddy of faintly glittering brass and ivory; and it was gone – vanished! Save for the lamp the table was bare.

Every one was silent for a minute. Then Filby said he was damned.

The Psychologist recovered from his stupor, and suddenly looked under the table. At that the Time Traveller laughed cheerfully. 'Well?' he said, with a reminiscence of the Psychologist. Then, getting up, he went to the tobacco jar on the mantel, and with his back to us began to fill his pipe.

We stared at each other. 'Look here,' said the Medical Man, 'are you in earnest about this? Do you seriously believe that that machine has travelled into time?'

'Certainly,' said the Time Traveller, stooping to light a spill at the fire. Then he turned, lighting his pipe, to look at the Psychologist's face. (The Psychologist, to show that he was not unhinged, helped himself to a cigar and tried to light it uncut.) 'What is more, I have a big machine nearly finished in there' – he indicated the laboratory – 'and when that is put together I mean to have a journey on my own account.'

'You mean to say that that machine has travelled into the future?' said Filby.

'Into the future or the past – I don't, for certain, know which.'

After an interval the Psychologist had an inspiration. 'It must have gone into the past if it has gone anywhere,' he said.

'Why?' said the Time Traveller.

'Because I presume that it has not moved in space, and if it travelled into the future it would still be here all this time, since it must have travelled through this time.'

'But,' said I, 'if it travelled into the past it would have been visible when we came first into this room; and last Thursday when we were here; and the Thursday before that; and so forth!'

'Serious objections,' remarked the Provincial Mayor, with an air of impartiality, turning towards the Time Traveller.

'Not a bit,' said the Time Traveller, and, to the Psychologist: 'You think. You can explain that. It's presentation below the threshold, you know, diluted presentation.'

'Of course,' said the Psychologist, and reassured us. 'That's a simple point of psychology. I should have thought of it. It's plain enough, and helps the paradox delightfully. We cannot see it, nor can we appreciate this machine, any more than we can the spoke of a wheel spinning, or a bullet flying through the air.

If it is travelling through time fifty times or a hundred times faster than we are, if it gets through a minute while we get through a second, the impression it creates will of course be only one-fiftieth or one-hundredth of what it would make if it were not travelling in time. That's plain enough.' He passed his hand through the space in which the machine had been. 'You see?' he said, laughing.

We sat and stared at the vacant table for a minute or so. Then the Time Traveller asked us what we thought of it all.

'It sounds plausible enough to-night,' said the Medical Man; 'but wait until to-morrow. Wait for the common sense of the morning.'

'Would you like to see the Time machine itself?' asked the Time Traveller. And therewith, taking the lamp in his hand, he led the way down the long, draughty corridor to his laboratory. I remember vividly the flickering light, his queer, broad head in silhouette, the dance of the shadows, how we all followed him, puzzled but incredulous, and how there in the laboratory we beheld a larger edition of the little mechanism which we had seen vanish from before our eyes. Parts were of nickel, parts of ivory, parts had certainly been filed or sawn out of rock crystal. The thing was generally complete, but the twisted crystalline bars lay unfinished upon the bench beside some sheets of drawings, and I took one up for a better look at it. Quartz it seemed to be.

'Look here,' said the Medical Man, 'are you perfectly serious? Or is this a trick – like that ghost you showed us last Christmas?'

'Upon that machine,' said the Time Traveller, holding the lamp aloft, 'I intend to explore time. Is that plain? I was never more serious in my life.'

None of us quite knew how to take it.

I caught Filby's eye over the shoulder of the Medical Man, and he winked at me solemnly.

§2

I think that at that time none of us quite believed in the Time Machine. The fact is, the Time Traveller was one of those men who are too clever to be believed: you never felt that you saw all round him; you always suspected some subtle reserve, some ingenuity in ambush, behind his lucid frankness. Had Filby shown the model and explained the matter in the Time Traveller's words, we should have shown *him* far less scepticism. For we should have perceived his motives: a pork butcher could understand Filby. But the Time Traveller had more than a touch of whim among his elements, and we distrusted him. Things that would have made the fame of a less clever man seemed tricks in his hands. It is a mistake to do things too easily. The serious people who took him seriously never felt quite sure of his deportment: they were somehow aware that trusting their reputations for judgment with him was like furnishing a nursery with egg-shell china. So I don't think any of us said very much about time travelling in the interval between that Thursday and the next, though its odd potentialities ran, no doubt, in most of our minds: its plausibility, that is, its practical incredibleness, the curious possibilities of anachronism and of utter confusion it suggested. For my own part, I was particularly preoccupied with the trick of the model. That I remember discussing with the Medical Man, whom I met on Friday at the Linnæan. He said he had seen a similar thing at Tübingen, and laid considerable stress on the blowing out of the candle. But how the trick was done he could not explain.

The next Thursday I went again to Richmond – I suppose I was one of the Time Traveller's most constant guests – and, arriving late, found four or five men already assembled in his drawing-room. The Medical Man was standing before the fire with a sheet of paper in one hand and his watch in the other. I looked round for the Time Traveller, and – 'It's half-past seven now,' said the Medical Man. 'I suppose we'd better have dinner?'

'Where's—?' said I, naming our host.

'You've just come? It's rather odd. He's unavoidably detained. He asks me in this note to lead off with dinner at seven if he's not back. Says he'll explain when he comes.'

'It seems a pity to let the dinner spoil,' said the Editor of a well-known daily paper; and thereupon the Doctor rang the bell.

The Psychologist was the only person besides the Doctor and myself who had attended the previous dinner. The other men were Blank, the Editor aforementioned, a certain journalist, and another – a quiet, shy man with a beard – whom I didn't know, and who, as far as my observation went, never opened his mouth all the evening. There was some speculation at the dinner-table about the Time Traveller's absence, and I suggested time travelling, in a half-jocular spirit. The Editor wanted that explained to him, and the Psychologist volunteered a wooden account of the 'ingenious paradox and trick' we had witnessed that day week. He was in the midst of his exposition when the door from the corridor opened slowly and without noise. I was facing the door, and saw it first. 'Hallo!' I said. 'At last!' And the door opened wider, and the Time Traveller stood before us. I gave a cry of surprise. 'Good heavens! man, what's the matter?' cried the Medical Man, who saw him next. And the whole tableful turned towards the door.

He was in an amazing plight. His coat was dusty and dirty, and smeared with green down the sleeves; his hair disordered, and as it seemed to me greyer – either with dust and dirt or because its colour had actually faded. His face was ghastly pale; his chin had a brown cut on it – a cut half healed; his expression was haggard and drawn, as by intense suffering. For a moment he hesitated in the doorway, as if he had been dazzled by the light. Then he came into the room. He walked with just such a limp as I have seen in footsore tramps. We stared at him in silence, expecting him to speak.

He said not a word, but came painfully to the table, and made a motion towards the wine. The Editor filled a glass of champagne, and pushed it towards him. He drained it, and it seemed to do him good: for he looked round the table, and the ghost of his old smile flickered across his face. 'What on earth have you been up to, man?' said the Doctor. The Time Traveller did not seem to hear. 'Don't let me disturb you,' he said, with a certain faltering articulation. 'I'm all right.' He stopped, held out his glass for more, and took it off at a draught. 'That's good,' he said. His eyes grew brighter, and a faint colour came into his cheeks. His glance flickered over our faces with a certain dull approval, and then went round the warm and comfortable room. Then he spoke again, still as it were feeling his way among his words. 'I'm going to wash and dress, and then I'll come down and explain things. . . . Save me some of that mutton. I'm starving for a bit of meat.'

He looked across at the Editor, who was a rare visitor, and hoped he was all right. The Editor began a question. 'Tell you presently,' said the Time Traveller. 'I'm – funny! Be all right in a minute.'

He put down his glass, and walked towards the staircase door. Again I remarked his lameness and the soft padding sound of his footfall, and standing up in my place, I saw his feet as he went out. He had nothing on them but a pair of tattered, blood-stained socks. Then the door closed upon him. I had half a mind to follow, till I remembered how he detested any fuss about himself. For a minute, perhaps, my mind was wool gathering. Then, 'Remarkable Behaviour of an Eminent Scientist,' I heard the Editor say, thinking (after his wont) in head-lines. And this brought my attention back to the bright dinner-table.

'What's the game?' said the Journalist. 'Has he been doing the Amateur Cadger? I don't follow.' I met the eye of the Psychologist, and read my own interpretation in his face. I thought of the Time Traveller limping painfully upstairs. I don't think any one else had noticed his lameness.

The first to recover completely from this surprise was the Medical Man, who rang the bell – the Time Traveller hated to have servants waiting at dinner – for a hot plate. At that the Editor turned to his knife and fork with a grunt, and the Silent Man followed suit. The dinner was resumed. Conversation was exclamatory for a little while, with gaps of wonderment; and then the Editor got fervent in his curiosity. 'Does our friend eke out his modest income with a crossing? or has he his Nebuchadnezzar phases?' he inquired. 'I feel assured it's this business of the Time Machine,' I said, and took up the Psychologist's account of our previous meeting. The new guests were frankly incredulous. The Editor raised objections. 'What *was* this time travelling? A man couldn't cover himself with dust by rolling in a paradox, could he?' And then, as the idea came home to him, he resorted to caricature. Hadn't they any clothes-brushes in the Future? The Journalist, too, would not believe at any price, and joined the Editor in the easy work of heaping ridicule on the whole thing. They were both the new kind of journalist – very joyous, irreverent young men. 'Our Special Correspondent in the Day after To-morrow reports,' the Journalist was saying – or rather shouting – when the Time Traveller came back. He was dressed in ordinary evening clothes, and nothing save his haggard look remained of the change that had startled me.

'I say,' said the Editor hilariously, 'these chaps here say you have been travelling into the middle of next week!! Tell us all about little Rosebery, will you? What will you take for the lot?'

The Time Traveller came to the place reserved for him without a word. He smiled quietly, in his old way. 'Where's my mutton?' he said. 'What a treat it is to stick a fork into meat again!'

'Story!' cried the Editor.

'Story be damned!' said the Time Traveller. 'I want something to eat. I won't say a word until I get some peptone into my arteries. Thanks. And the salt.'

'One word,' said I. 'Have you been time travelling?'

'Yes,' said the Time Traveller, with his mouth full, nodding his head.

'I'd give a shilling a line for a verbatim note,' said the Editor. The Time Traveller pushed his glass towards the Silent Man and rang it with his fingernail; at which the Silent Man, who had been staring at his face, started convulsively, and poured him wine. The rest of the dinner was uncomfortable. For my own part, sudden questions kept on rising to my lips, and I dare say it was the same with the others. The Journalist tried to relieve the tension by telling anecdotes of Hettie Potter. The Time Traveller devoted his attention to his dinner, and displayed the appetite of a tramp. The Medical Man smoked a cigarette, and watched the Time Traveller through his eyelashes. The Silent Man seemed even more clumsy than usual, and drank champagne with regularity and determination out of sheer nervousness. At last the Time Traveller pushed his plate away, and looked round us. 'I suppose I must apologize,' he said. 'I was simply starving. I've had a most amazing time.' He reached out his hand for a cigar, and cut the end. 'But come into the smoking-room. It's too long a story to tell over greasy plates.'

And ringing the bell in passing, he led the way into the adjoining room.

'You have told Blank, and Dash, and Chose about the machine?' he said to me, leaning back in his easy-chair and naming the three new guests.

'But the thing's a mere paradox,' said the Editor.

'I can't argue tonight. I don't mind telling you the story, but I can't argue. I will,' he went on, 'tell you the story of what has happened to me, if you like, but you must refrain from interruptions. I want to tell it. Badly. Most of it will sound like lying. So be it! It's true – every word of it, all the same. I was in my laboratory at four o'clock, and since then ... I've lived eight days ... such days as no human being ever lived before! I'm nearly worn out, but I shan't sleep till I've told this thing over to you. Then I shall go to bed. But no interruptions! Is it agreed?'

'Agreed,' said the Editor, and the rest of us echoed 'Agreed.' And with that the Time Traveller began his story as I have set it forth. He sat back in his chair at first, and spoke like a weary man. Afterwards he got more animated. In writing it down I feel with only too much keenness the inadequacy of pen and ink – and, above all, my own inadequacy – to express its quality. You read, I will suppose, attentively enough; but you cannot see the speaker's white, sincere face in the bright circle of the little lamp, nor hear the intonation of his voice. You cannot know how his expression followed the turns of his story! Most of us hearers were in shadow, for the candles in the smoking-room had not been lighted, and only the face of the Journalist and the legs of the Silent Man from the knees downward were illuminated. At first we glanced now and again at each other. After a time we ceased to do that, and looked only at the Time Traveller's face.

3

'I told some of you last Thursday of the principles of the Time Machine, and showed you the actual thing itself, incomplete in the workshop. There it is now, a little travel-worn, truly; and one of the ivory bars is cracked, and a brass rail bent; but the rest of it's sound enough. I expected to finish it on Friday; but on Friday, when the putting together was nearly done, I found that one of the nickel bars was exactly one inch too short, and this I had to get remade; so that the thing was not complete until this morning. It was at ten o'clock to-day that the first of all Time Machines began its career. I gave it a last tap, tried all the screws again, put one more drop of oil on the quartz rod, and sat myself in the saddle. I suppose a suicide who holds a pistol to his skull feels much the same wonder at what will come next as I felt then. I took the starting lever in one hand and the stopping one in the other, pressed the first, and almost immediately the second. I seemed to reel; I felt a nightmare sensation of falling; and, looking round, I saw the laboratory exactly as before. Had anything happened? For a moment I suspected that my intellect had tricked me. Then I noted the clock. A moment before, as it seemed, it had stood at a minute or so past ten; now it was nearly half-past three!

'I drew a breath, set my teeth, gripped the starting lever with both hands, and went off with a thud. The laboratory got hazy and went dark. Mrs. Watchett came in and walked, apparently without seeing me, towards the garden door. I suppose it took her a minute or so to traverse the place, but to me she seemed to shoot across the room like a rocket. I pressed the lever over to its extreme position. The night came like the turning out of a lamp, and in another moment came to-morrow. The laboratory grew faint and hazy, then fainter and ever fainter. To-morrow night came black, then day again, night again, day again, faster and faster still. An eddying murmur filled my ears, and a strange, dumb confusedness descended on my mind.

'I am afraid I cannot convey the peculiar sensations of time travelling. They are excessively unpleasant. There is a feeling exactly like that one has upon a switchback – of a helpless headlong motion! I felt the same horrible anticipation, too, of an imminent smash. As I put on pace, night followed day like the flapping of a black wing. The dim suggestion of the laboratory seemed presently to fall away from me, and I saw the sun hopping swiftly across the sky, leaping it every minute, and every minute marking a day. I supposed the laboratory had been destroyed and I had come into the open air. I had a dim impression of scaffolding, but I was already going too fast to be conscious of any moving things. The slowest snail that ever crawled dashed by too fast for me. The twinkling succession of darkness and light was excessively painful to the eye. Then, in the intermittent darknesses, I saw the moon spinning swiftly through her quarters from new to full, and had a faint glimpse of the circling stars. Presently, as I went on, still gaining velocity, the palpitation of night and day merged into one continuous greyness; the sky took on a wonderful deepness of blue, a splendid luminous colour like that of early twilight; the jerking sun became a streak of fire, a brilliant arch, in space; the moon a fainter fluctuating band; and I could see nothing of the stars, save now and then a brighter circle flickering in the blue.

'The landscape was misty and vague. I was still on the hill-side upon which this house now stands, and the shoulder rose above me grey and dim. I saw trees growing and changing like puffs of vapour, now brown, now green; they grew, spread, shivered, and passed away. I saw huge buildings rise up faint and fair, and pass like dreams. The whole surface of the earth seemed changed – melting and flowing under my eyes. The little hands upon the dials that registered my speed raced round faster and faster. Presently I noted that the sun belt swayed up and down, from solstice to solstice, in a minute or less, and that consequently my pace was over a year a minute; and minute by minute the white snow flashed across the world, and vanished, and was followed by the bright, brief green of spring.

'The unpleasant sensations of the start were less poignant now. They merged at last into a kind of hysterical exhilaration. I remarked indeed a clumsy swaying of the machine, for which I was unable to account. But my mind was too confused to attend to it, so with a kind of madness growing upon me, I flung myself into futurity. At first I scarce thought of stopping, scarce thought of anything but these new sensations. But presently a fresh series of impressions grew up in my mind – a certain curiosity and therewith a certain dread – until at last they took complete possession of me. What strange developments of humanity, what wonderful advances upon our rudimentary civilization, I thought, might not appear when I came to look nearly into the dim elusive world that raced and fluctuated before my eyes! I saw great and splendid architecture rising about me, more massive than any buildings of our own time, and yet, as it seemed, built of glimmer and mist. I saw a richer green flow up the hillside, and remain there without any wintry intermission. Even through the veil of my confusion the earth seemed very fair. And so my mind came round to the business of stopping.

'The peculiar risk lay in the possibility of my finding some substance in the space which I, or the machine, occupied. So long as I travelled at a high velocity through time, this scarcely mattered; I was, so to speak, attenuated – was slipping like a vapour through the interstices of intervening substances! But to come to a stop involved the jamming of myself, molecule by molecule, into whatever lay in my way; meant bringing my atoms into such intimate contact with those of the obstacle that a profound chemical reaction – possibly a far-reaching explosion – would result, and blow myself and my apparatus out of all possible dimensions – into the Unknown. This possibility had occurred to me again and again while I was making the machine; but then I had cheerfully accepted it as an unavoidable risk – one of the risks a man has got to take! Now the risk was inevitable, I no longer saw it in the same cheerful light. The fact is that, insensibly, the absolute strangeness of everything, the sickly jarring and swaying of the machine, above all, the feeling of prolonged falling, had absolutely upset my nerve. I told myself that I could never stop, and with a gust of petulance I resolved to stop forthwith. Like an impatient fool, I lugged over the lever, and incontinently the thing went reeling over, and I was flung headlong through the air.

'There was the sound of a clap of thunder in my ears. I may have been stunned for a moment. A pitiless hail was hissing round me, and I was sitting on soft turf in front of the overset machine. Everything still seemed grey, but presently I remarked that the confusion in my ears was gone. I looked round me. I was on what seemed to be a little lawn in a garden, surrounded by rhododendron bushes, and I noticed that their mauve and purple blossoms were dropping in a shower under the beating of the hailstones. The rebounding, dancing hail hung in a cloud over the machine, and drove along the ground like smoke. In a moment I was wet to the skin. "Fine hospitality," said I, "to a man who has travelled innumerable years to see you."

'Presently I thought what a fool I was to get wet. I stood up and looked round me. A colossal figure, carved apparently in some white stone, loomed indistinctly beyond the rhododendrons through the hazy downpour. But all else of the world was invisible.

'My sensations would be hard to describe. As the columns of hail grew thinner, I saw the white figure more distinctly. It was very large, for a silver birch-tree touched its shoulder. It was of white marble, in shape something like a winged sphinx, but the wings, instead of being carried vertically at the sides, were spread so that it seemed to hover. The pedestal, it appeared to me, was of bronze, and was thick with verdigris. It chanced that the face was towards me; the sightless eyes seemed to watch me; there was the faint shadow of a smile on the lips. It was greatly weather-worn, and that imparted an unpleasant suggestion of disease. I stood looking at it for a little space – half a minute, perhaps, or half an hour. It seemed to advance and to recede as the hail drove before it denser or thinner. At last I tore my eyes from it for a moment, and saw that the hail curtain had worn threadbare, and that the sky was lightening with the promise of the sun.

'I looked up again at the crouching white shape, and the full temerity of my voyage came suddenly upon me. What might appear when that hazy curtain was altogether withdrawn? What might not have happened to men? What if cruelty had grown into a common passion? What if in this interval the race had lost its manliness, and had developed into something inhuman, unsympathetic, and overwhelmingly powerful? I might seem some old-world savage animal, only the more dreadful and disgusting for our common likeness – a foul creature to be incontinently slain.

'Already I saw other vast shapes – huge buildings with intricate parapets and tall columns, with a wooded hillside dimly creeping in upon me through the lessening storm. I was seized with a panic fear. I turned frantically to the Time Machine, and strove hard to readjust it. As I did so the shafts of the sun smote through the thunderstorm. The grey downpour was swept aside and vanished like the trailing garments of a ghost. Above me, in the intense blue of the summer sky, some faint brown shreds of cloud whirled into nothingness. The great buildings about me stood out clear and distinct, shining with the wet of the thunderstorm, and picked out in white by the unmelted hail-stones piled along their courses. I felt naked in a strange world. I felt as perhaps a bird may feel in the clear air, knowing the hawk wings above and will swoop. My fear grew to frenzy. I took a breathing space, set my teeth, and again grappled fiercely, wrist and knee, with the machine. It gave under my desperate onset and turned over. It struck my chin violently. One hand on the saddle, the other on the lever, I stood panting heavily in attitude to mount again.

'But with this recovery of a prompt retreat my courage recovered. I looked more curiously and less fearfully at this world of the remote future. In a circular opening, high up in the wall of the nearer house, I saw a group of figures clad in rich soft robes. They had seen me, and their faces were directed towards me.

'Then I heard voices approaching me. Coming through the bushes by the White Sphinx were the heads and shoulders of men running. One of these emerged in a pathway leading straight to the little lawn upon which I stood with my machine. He was a slight creature – perhaps four feet high – clad in a purple tunic, girdled at the waist with a leather belt. Sandals or buskins – I could not clearly distinguish which – were on his feet; his legs were bare to the knees, and his head was bare. Noticing that, I noticed for the first time how warm the air was.

'He struck me as being a very beautiful and graceful creature, but indescribably frail. His flushed face reminded me of the more beautiful kind of consumptive – that hectic beauty of which we used to hear so much. At the sight of him I suddenly regained confidence. I took my hands from the machine.

4

'In another moment we were standing face to face, I and this fragile thing out of futurity. He came straight up to me and laughed into my eyes. The absence from his bearing of any sign of fear struck me at once. Then he turned to the two others who were following him and spoke to them in a strange and very sweet and liquid tongue.

'There were others coming, and presently a little group of perhaps eight or ten of these exquisite creatures were about me. One of them addressed me. It came into my head, oddly enough, that my voice was too harsh and deep for them. So I shook my head, and, pointing to my ears, shook it again. He came a step forward, hesitated, and then touched my hand. Then I felt other soft little tentacles upon my back and shoulders. They wanted to make sure I was real. There was nothing in this at all alarming. Indeed, there was something in these pretty little people that inspired confidence – a graceful gentleness, a certain childlike ease. And besides, they looked so frail that I could fancy myself flinging the whole dozen of them about like nine-pins. But I made a sudden motion to warn them when I saw their little pink hands feeling at the Time Machine. Happily then, when it was not too late, I thought of a danger I had hitherto forgotten, and reaching over the bars of the machine I unscrewed the little levers that would set it in motion, and put these in my pocket. Then I turned again to see what I could do in the way of communication.

'And then, looking more nearly into their features, I saw some further peculiarities in their Dresden china type of prettiness. Their hair, which was uniformly curly, came to a sharp end at the neck and cheek; there was not the faintest suggestion of it on the face, and their ears were singularly minute. The mouths were small, with bright red, rather thin lips, and the little chins ran to a point. The eyes were large and mild; and – this may seem egotism on my part – I fancied even then that there was a certain lack of the interest I might have expected in them.

'As they made no effort to communicate with me, but simply stood round me smiling and speaking in soft cooing notes to each other, I began the conversation. I pointed to the Time Machine and to myself. Then hesitating for a moment how to express time, I pointed to the sun. At once a quaintly pretty little figure in chequered purple and white followed my gesture, and then astonished me by imitating the sound of thunder.

'For a moment I was staggered, though the import of his gesture was plain enough. The question had come into my mind abruptly: were these creatures fools? You may hardly understand how it took me. You see I had always anticipated that the people of the year Eight Hundred and Two Thousand odd would be incredibly in front of us in knowledge, art, everything. Then one of them suddenly asked me a question that showed him to be on the intellectual level of one of our five-year-old children – asked me, in fact, if I had come from the sun in a thunderstorm! It let loose the judgment I had suspended upon their clothes, their frail light limbs, and fragile features. A flow of disappointment rushed across my mind. For a moment I felt that I had built the Time Machine in vain.

'I nodded, pointed to the sun, and gave them such a vivid rendering of a thunderclap as startled them. They all withdrew a pace or so and bowed. Then came one laughing towards me, carrying a chain of beautiful flowers altogether new to me, and put it about my neck. The idea was received with melodious applause; and presently they were all running to and fro for flowers, and laughingly flinging them upon me until I was almost smothered with blossom. You who have never seen the like can scarcely imagine what delicate and wonderful flowers countless years of culture had created. Then someone suggested that their plaything should be exhibited in the nearest building, and so I was led past the sphinx of white marble, which had seemed to watch me all the while with a smile at my astonishment, towards a vast grey edifice of fretted stone. As I went with them the memory of my confident anticipations of a profoundly grave and intellectual posterity came, with irresistible merriment, to my mind.

'The building had a huge entry, and was altogether of colossal dimensions. I was naturally most occupied with the growing

crowd of little people, and with the big open portals that
yawned before me shadowy and mysterious. My general
impression of the world I saw over their heads was of a tangled
waste of beautiful bushes and flowers, a long-neglected and yet
weedless garden. I saw a number of tall spikes of strange white
flowers, measuring a foot perhaps across the spread of the
waxen petals. They grew scattered, as if wild, among the
variegated shrubs, but, as I say, I did not examine them closely
at this time. The Time Machine was left deserted on the turf
among the rhododendrons.

'The arch of the doorway was richly carved, but naturally I
did not observe the carving very narrowly, though I fancied I
saw suggestions of old Phoenician decorations as I passed
through, and it struck me that they were very badly broken and
weather-worn. Several more brightly clad people met me in the
doorway, and so we entered, I, dressed in dingy nineteenth-
century garments, looking grotesque enough, garlanded with
flowers, and surrounded by an eddying mass of bright, soft-
coloured robes and shining white limbs, in a melodious whirl of
laughter and laughing speech.

'The big doorway opened into a proportionately great hall
hung with brown. The roof was in shadow, and the windows,
partially glazed with coloured glass and partially unglazed,
admitted a tempered light. The floor was made up of huge
blocks of some very hard white metal, not plates nor slabs –
blocks, and it was so much worn, as I judged by the going to
and fro of past generations, as to be deeply channelled along the
more frequented ways. Transverse to the length were innumerable tables made of slabs of polished stone, raised perhaps a
foot from the floor, and upon these were heaps of fruits. Some I
recognized as a kind of hypertrophied raspberry and orange, but
for the most part they were strange.

'Between the tables was scattered a great number of cushions.
Upon these my conductors seated themselves, signing for me to
do likewise. With a pretty absence of ceremony they began to
eat the fruit with their hands, flinging peel and stalks and so
forth, into the round openings in the sides of the tables. I was
not loth to follow their example, for I felt thirsty and hungry.
As I did so I surveyed the hall at my leisure.

'And perhaps the thing that struck me most was its dilapidated
look. The stained-glass windows, which displayed only a geo-

metrical pattern, were broken in many places, and the curtains that hung across the lower end were thick with dust. And it caught my eye that the corner of the marble table near me was fractured. Nevertheless, the general effect was extremely rich and picturesque. There were, perhaps, a couple of hundred people dining in the hall, and most of them, seated as near to me as they could come, were watching me with interest, their little eyes shining over the fruit they were eating. All were clad in the same soft, and yet strong, silky material.

'Fruit, by the bye, was all their diet. These people of the remote future were strict vegetarians, and while I was with them, in spite of some carnal cravings, I had to be frugivorous also. Indeed, I found afterwards that horses, cattle, sheep, dogs, had followed the Ichthyosaurus into extinction. But the fruits were very delightful; one, in particular, that seemed to be in season all the time I was there – a floury thing in a three-sided husk – was especially good, and I made it my staple. At first I was puzzled by all these strange fruits, and by the strange flowers I saw, but later I began to perceive their import.

'However, I am telling you of my fruit dinner in the distant future now. So soon as my appetite was a little checked, I determined to make a resolute attempt to learn the speech of these new men of mine. Clearly that was the next thing to do. The fruits seemed a convenient thing to begin upon, and holding one of these up I began a series of interrogative sounds and gestures. I had some considerable difficulty in conveying my meaning. At first my efforts met with a stare of surprise or inextinguishable laughter, but presently a fair-haired little creature seemed to grasp my intention and repeated a name. They had to chatter and explain the business at great length to each other, and my first attempts to make the exquisite little sounds of their language caused an immense amount of amusement. However, I felt like a schoolmaster amidst children, and persisted, and presently I had a score of noun substantives at least at my command; and then I got to demonstrative pronouns, and even the verb "to eat". But it was slow work, and the little people soon tired and wanted to get away from my interrogations, so I determined, rather of necessity, to let them give their lessons in little doses when they felt inclined. And very little doses I found they were before long, for I never met people more indolent or more easily fatigued.

'A queer thing I soon discovered about my little hosts, and that was their lack of interest. They would come to me with eager cries of astonishment, like children, but like children they would soon stop examining me and wander away after some other toy. The dinner and my conversational beginnings ended, I noted for the first time that almost all those who had surrounded me at first were gone. It is odd, too, how speedily I came to disregard these little people. I went out through the portal into the sunlit world again so soon as my hunger was satisfied. I was continually meeting more of these men of the future, who would follow me a little distance, chatter and laugh about me, and, having smiled and gesticulated in a friendly way, leave me again to my own devices.

'The calm of evening was upon the world as I emerged from the great hall, and the scene was lit by the warm glow of the setting sun. At first things were very confusing. Everything was so entirely different from the world I had known – even the flowers. The big building I had left was situated on the slope of a broad river valley, but the Thames had shifted, perhaps, a mile from its present position. I resolved to mount to the summit of a crest, perhaps a mile and a half away, from which I could get a wider view of this our planet in the year Eight Hundred and Two Thousand Seven Hundred and One A.D. For that, I should explain, was the date the little dials of my machine recorded.

'As I walked I was watchful for every impression that could possibly help to explain the condition of ruinous splendour in which I found the world – for ruinous it was. A little way up the hill, for instance, was a great heap of granite, bound together by masses of aluminium, a vast labyrinth of precipitous walls and crumbled heaps, amidst which were thick heaps of very beautiful pagoda-like plants – nettles possibly – but wonderfully tinted with brown about the leaves, and incapable of stinging. It was evidently the derelict remains of some vast structure, to what end built I could not determine. It was here that I was destined, at a later date, to have a very strange experience – the first intimation of a still stranger discovery – but of that I will speak in its proper place.

'Looking round with a sudden thought, from a terrace on which I rested for a while, I realized that there were no small houses to be seen. Apparently the single house, and possibly even the household, had vanished. Here and there among the greenery were palace-like buildings, but the house and the cottage, which form such characteristic features of our own English landscape, had disappeared.

'"Communism," said I to myself.

'And on the heels of that came another thought. I looked at the half-dozen little figures that were following me. Then, in a flash, I perceived that all had the same form of costume, the same soft hairless visage, and the same girlish rotundity of limb. It may seem strange, perhaps, that I had not noticed this before. But everything was so strange. Now, I saw the fact plainly enough. In costume, and in all the differences of texture and bearing that now mark off the sexes from each other, these people of the future were alike. And the children seemed to my eyes to be but the miniatures of their parents. I judged, then, that the children of that time were extremely precocious, physically at least, and I found afterwards abundant verification of my opinion.

'Seeing the ease and security in which these people were living, I felt that this close resemblance of the sexes was after all what one would expect; for the strength of a man and the softness of a woman, the institution of the family, and the differentiation of occupations are mere militant necessities of an age of physical force. Where population is balanced and abundant, much child-bearing becomes an evil rather than a blessing to the State; where violence comes but rarely and offspring are secure, there is less necessity – indeed there is no necessity – for an efficient family, and the specialization of the sexes with reference to their children's needs disappears. We see some beginnings of this even in our own time, and in this future age it was complete. This, I must remind you, was my speculation at the time. Later, I was to appreciate how far it fell short of the reality.

'While I was musing upon these things, my attention was attracted by a pretty little structure, like a well under a cupola. I thought in a transitory way of the oddness of wells still existing, and then resumed the thread of my speculations. There were no large buildings towards the top of the hill, and as my walking powers were evidently miraculous, I was presently left alone for the first time. With a strange sense of freedom and adventure I pushed on up to the crest.

'There I found a seat of some yellow metal that I did not recognize, corroded in places with a kind of pinkish rust and half smothered in soft moss, the armrests cast and filed into the resemblance of griffins' heads. I sat down on it, and I surveyed the broad view of our world under the sunset of that long day. It was as sweet and fair a view as I have ever seen. The sun had already gone below the horizon and the west was flaming gold, touched with some horizontal bars of purple and crimson. Below was the valley of the Thames, in which the river lay like a band of burnished steel. I have already spoken of the great palaces dotted about among the variegated greenery, some in ruins and some still occupied. Here and there rose a white or silvery figure in the waste garden of the earth, here and there came the sharp vertical line of some cupola or obelisk. There were no hedges, no signs of proprietary rights, no evidences of agriculture; the whole earth had become a garden.

'So watching, I began to put my interpretation upon the things I had seen, and as it shaped itself to me that evening, my interpretation was something in this way. (Afterwards I found I had got only a half-truth – or only a glimpse of one facet of the truth.)

'It seemed to me that I had happened upon humanity upon the wane. The ruddy sunset set me thinking of the sunset of mankind. For the first time I began to realize an odd consequence of the social effort in which we are at present engaged. And yet, come to think, it is a logical consequence enough. Strength is the outcome of need; security sets a premium on feebleness. The work of ameliorating the conditions of life – the true civilizing process that makes life more and more secure – had gone steadily on to a climax. One triumph of a united humanity over Nature had followed another. Things that are now mere dreams had become projects deliberately put in hand and carried forward. And the harvest was what I saw!

'After all, the sanitation and the agriculture of to-day are still in the rudimentary stage. The science of our time has attacked but a little department of the field of human disease, but, even so, it spreads its operations very steadily and persistently. Our agriculture and horticulture destroy a weed just here and there and cultivate perhaps a score or so of wholesome plants, leaving the greater number to fight out a balance as they can. We improve our favourite plants and animals – and how few they are – gradually by selective breeding; now a new and better peach, now a seedless grape, now a sweeter and larger flower, now a more convenient breed of cattle. We improve them gradually, because our ideals are vague and tentative, and our knowledge is very limited; because Nature, too, is shy and slow in our clumsy hands. Some day all this will be better organized, and still better. That is the drift of the current in spite of the eddies. The whole world will be intelligent, educated, and co-operating; things will move faster and faster towards the subjugation of Nature. In the end, wisely and carefully we shall readjust the balance of animal and vegetable life to suit our human needs.

'This adjustment, I say, must have been done, and done well; done indeed for all Time, in the space of Time across which my machine had leaped. The air was free from gnats, the earth from weeds or fungi; everywhere were fruits and sweet and delightful flowers; brilliant butterflies flew hither and thither. The ideal of preventive medicine was attained. Diseases had been stamped out. I saw no evidence of any contagious diseases during all my stay. And I shall have to tell you later that even the processes of putrefaction and decay had been profoundly affected by these changes.

'Social triumphs, too, had been effected. I saw mankind housed in splendid shelters, gloriously clothed, and as yet I had found them engaged in no toil. There were no signs of struggle, neither social nor economical struggle. The shop, the advertisement, traffic, all that commerce which constitutes the body of our world, was gone. It was natural on that golden evening that I should jump at the idea of a social paradise. The difficulty of increasing population had been met, I guessed, and population had ceased to increase.

'But with this change in condition comes inevitably adaptations to the change. What, unless biological science is a mass of errors, is the cause of human intelligence and vigour? Hardship and freedom: conditions under which the active, strong, and subtle survive and the weaker go to the wall; conditions that put a premium upon the loyal alliance of capable men, upon self-restraint, patience, and decision. And the institution of the family, and the emotions that arise therein, the fierce jealousy, the tenderness for offspring, parental self-devotion, all found their justification and support in the imminent dangers of the young. *Now*, where are these imminent dangers? There is a sentiment arising, and it will grow, against connubial jealousy, against fierce maternity, against passion of all sorts; unnecessary things now, and things that make us uncomfortable, savage survivals, discords in a refined and pleasant life.

'I thought of the physical slightness of the people, their lack of intelligence, and those big abundant ruins, and it strengthened my belief in a perfect conquest of Nature. For after the battle comes Quiet. Humanity had been strong, energetic, and intelligent, and had used all its abundant vitality to alter the conditions under which it lived. And now came the reaction of the altered conditions.

'Under the new conditions of perfect comfort and security, that restless energy, that with us is strength, would become weakness. Even in our own time certain tendencies and desires, once necessary to survival, are a constant source of failure. Physical courage and the love of battle, for instance, are no great help – may even be hindrances – to a civilised man. And in a state of physical balance and security, power, intellectual as well as physical, would be out of place. For countless years I judged there had been no danger of war or solitary violence, no danger from wild beasts, no wasting disease to require strength of constitution, no need of toil. For such a life, what we should call the weak are as well equipped as the strong, are indeed no longer weak. Better equipped indeed they are, for the strong would be fretted by an energy for which there was no outlet. No doubt the exquisite beauty of the buildings I saw was the outcome of the last surgings of the now purposeless energy of mankind before it settled down into perfect harmony with the conditions under which it lived – the flourish of that triumph which began the last great peace. This has ever been the fate of energy in security; it takes to art and to eroticism, and then come languor and decay.

'Even this artistic impetus would at last die away – had almost died in the Time I saw. To adorn themselves with flowers, to dance, to sing in the sunlight; so much was left of the artistic spirit, and no more. Even that would fade in the end into a contented inactivity. We are kept keen on the grindstone of pain and necessity, and, it seemed to me, that here was that hateful grindstone broken at last!

'As I stood there in the gathering dark I thought that in this simple explanation I had mastered the problem of the world – mastered the whole secret of these delicious people. Possibly the checks they had devised for the increase of population had succeeded too well, and their numbers had rather diminished than kept stationary. That would account for the abandoned ruins. Very simple was my explanation, and plausible enough – as most wrong theories are!

'As I stood there musing over this too perfect triumph of man, the full moon, yellow and gibbous, came up out of an overflow of silver light in the north-east. The bright little figures ceased to move about below, a noiseless owl flitted by, and I shivered with the chill of the night. I determined to descend and find where I could sleep.

'I looked for the building I knew. Then my eye travelled along to the figure of the White Sphinx upon the pedestal of bronze, growing distinct as the light of the rising moon grew brighter. I could see the silver birch against it. There was the tangle of rhododendron bushes, black in the pale light, and there was the little lawn. I looked at the lawn again. A queer doubt chilled my complacency. "No," said I stoutly to myself, "that was not the lawn."

'But it *was* the lawn. For the white leprous face of the sphinx was towards it. Can you imagine what I felt as this conviction came home to me? But you cannot. The Time Machine was gone!

'At once, like a lash across the face, came the possibility of losing my own age, of being left helpless in this strange new world. The bare thought of it was an actual physical sensation. I could feel it grip me at the throat and stop my breathing. In another moment I was in a passion of fear and running with great leaping strides down the slope. Once I fell headlong and cut my face; I lost no time in stanching the blood, but jumped up and ran on, with a warm trickle down my cheek and chin. All the time I ran I was saying to myself: "They have moved it a little, pushed it under the bushes out of the way." Nevertheless, I ran with all my might. All the time, with the certainty that sometimes comes with excessive dread, I knew that such assurance was folly, knew instinctively that the machine was removed out of my reach. My breath came with pain. I suppose I covered the whole distance from the hill crest to the little lawn, two miles, perhaps, in ten minutes. And I am not a young man. I cursed aloud, as I ran, at my confident folly in leaving the machine, wasting good breath thereby. I cried aloud, and none answered. Not a creature seemed to be stirring in that moonlit world.

'When I reached the lawn my worst fears were realized. Not a trace of the thing was to be seen. I felt faint and cold when I faced the empty space among the black tangle of bushes. I ran round it furiously, as if the thing might be hidden in a corner, and then stopped abruptly, with my hands clutching my hair. Above me towered the sphinx, upon the bronze pedestal, white, shining, leprous, in the light of the rising moon. It seemed to smile in mockery of my dismay.

'I might have consoled myself by imagining the little people had put the mechanism in some shelter for me, had I not felt assured of their physical and intellectual inadequacy. That is what dismayed me: the sense of some hitherto unsuspected power, through whose intervention my invention had vanished. Yet, of one thing I felt assured: unless some other age had produced its exact duplicate, the machine could not have moved in time. The attachment of the levers – I will show you the method later – prevented any one from tampering with it in that way when they were removed. It had moved, and was hid, only in space. But then, where could it be?

'I think I must have had a kind of frenzy. I remember running violently in and out among the moonlit bushes all round the sphinx, and startling some white animal that, in the dim light, I took for a small deer. I remember, too, late that night, beating the bushes with my clenched fists until my knuckles were gashed and bleeding from the broken twigs. Then, sobbing and raving in my anguish of mind, I went down to the great building of stone. The big hall was dark, silent, and deserted. I slipped on the uneven floor, and fell over one of the malachite tables, almost breaking my shin. I lit a match and went on past the dusty curtains, of which I have told you.

'There I found a second great hall covered with cushions, upon which, perhaps, a score or so of the little people were sleeping. I have no doubt they found my second appearance strange enough, coming suddenly out of the quiet darkness with inarticulate noises and the splutter and flare of a match. For they had forgotten about matches. "Where is my Time

Machine?" I began, bawling like an angry child, laying hands upon them and shaking them up together. It must have been very queer to them. Some laughed, most of them looked sorely frightened. When I saw them standing round me, it came into my head that I was doing as foolish a thing as it was possible for me to do under the circumstances, in trying to revive the sensation of fear. For, reasoning from their daylight behaviour, I thought that fear must be forgotten.

'Abruptly, I dashed down the match, and, knocking one of the people over in my course, went blundering across the big dining-hall again, out under the moonlight. I heard cries of terror and their little feet running and stumbling this way and that. I do not remember all I did as the moon crept up the sky. I suppose it was the unexpected nature of my loss that maddened me. I felt hopelessly cut off from my own kind – a strange animal in an unknown world. I must have raved to and fro, screaming and crying upon God and Fate. I have a memory of horrible fatigue, as the long night of despair wore away; of looking in this impossible place and that; of groping among moonlit ruins and touching strange creatures in the black shadows; at last, of lying on the ground near the sphinx and weeping with absolute wretchedness. I had nothing left but misery. Then I slept, and when I woke again it was full day, and a couple of sparrows were hopping round me on the turf within reach of my arm.

'I sat up in the freshness of the morning, trying to remember how I had got there, and why I had such a profound sense of desertion and despair. Then things came clear in my mind. With the plain, reasonable daylight, I could look my circumstances fairly in the face. I saw the wild folly of my frenzy overnight, and I could reason with myself. "Suppose the worst?" I said. "Suppose the machine altogether lost – perhaps destroyed? It behoves me to be calm and patient, to learn the way of the people, to get a clear idea of the method of my loss, and the means of getting materials and tools; so that in the end, perhaps, I may make another." That would be my only hope, a poor hope perhaps, but better than despair. And, after all, it was a beautiful and curious world.

'But probably the machine had only been taken away. Still, I must be calm and patient, find its hiding-place, and recover it by force or cunning. And with that I scrambled to my feet and looked about me, wondering where I could bathe. I felt weary, stiff, and travel-soiled. The freshness of the morning made me desire an equal freshness. I had exhausted my emotion. Indeed, as I went about my business, I found myself wondering at my intense excitement overnight. I made a careful examination of the ground about the little lawn. I wasted some time in futile questionings, conveyed, as well as I was able, to such of the little people as came by. They all failed to understand my gestures; some were simply stolid, some thought it was a jest and laughed at me. I had the hardest task in the world to keep my hands off their pretty laughing faces. It was a foolish impulse, but the devil begotten of fear and blind anger was ill curbed and still eager to take advantage of my perplexity. The turf gave better counsel. I found a groove ripped in it, about midway between the pedestal of the sphinx and the marks of my feet where, on arrival, I had struggled with the overturned machine. There were other signs of removal about, with queer narrow footprints like those I could imagine made by a sloth. This directed my closer attention to the pedestal. It was, as I think I have said, of bronze. It was not a mere block, but highly decorated with deep framed panels on either side. I went and rapped at these. The pedestal was hollow. Examining the panels with care I found them discontinuous with the frames. There were no handles or keyholes, but possibly the panels, if they were doors, as I supposed, opened from within. One thing was clear enough to my mind. It took no very great mental effort to infer that my Time Machine was inside that pedestal. But how it got there was a different problem.

'I saw the heads of two orange-clad people coming through the bushes and under some blossom-covered apple-trees towards me. I turned smiling to them and beckoned them to me. They came, and then, pointing to the bronze pedestal, I tried to intimate my wish to open it. But at my first gesture towards this they behaved very oddly. I don't know how to convey their expression to you. Suppose you were to use a grossly improper gesture to a delicate-minded woman – it is how she would look. They went off as if they had received the last possible insult. I tried a sweet-looking little chap in white next, with exactly the same result. Somehow, his manner made me feel ashamed of myself. But, as you know, I wanted the Time Machine, and I tried him once more. As he turned off, like the others, my temper got the better of me. In three strides I was after him, had him by the loose part of his robe round the neck, and began dragging him towards the sphinx. Then I saw the horror and repugnance of his face, and all of a sudden I let him go.

'But I was not beaten yet. I banged with my fist at the bronze panels. I thought I heard something stir inside – to be explicit, I thought I heard a sound like a chuckle – but I must have been mistaken. Then I got a big pebble from the river, and came and hammered till I had flattened a coil in the decorations, and the verdigris came off in powdery flakes. The delicate little people must have heard me hammering in gusty outbreaks a mile away on either hand, but nothing came of it. I saw a crowd of them upon the slopes, looking furtively at me. At last, hot and tired, I sat down to watch the place. But I was too restless to watch long; I am too Occidental for a long vigil. I could work at a problem for years, but to wait inactive for twenty-four hours – that is another matter.

'I got up after a time, and began walking aimlessly through the bushes towards the hill again. "Patience," said I to myself. "If you want your machine again you must leave that sphinx alone. If they mean to take your machine away, it's little good your wrecking their bronze panels, and if they don't, you will get it back as soon as you can ask for it. To sit among all those unknown things before a puzzle like that is hopeless. That way lies monomania. Face this world. Learn its ways, watch it, be careful of too hasty guesses at its meaning. In the end you will find clues to it all." Then suddenly the humour of the situation came into my mind: the thought of the years I had spent in study and toil to get into the future age, and now my passion of anxiety to get out of it. I had made myself the most complicated and the most hopeless trap that ever a man devised. Although it was at my own expense, I could not help myself. I laughed aloud.

'Going through the big palace, it seemed to me that the little people avoided me. It may have been my fancy, or it may have had something to do with my hammering at the gates of bronze. Yet I felt tolerably sure of the avoidance. I was careful, however, to show no concern and to abstain from any pursuit of them, and in the course of a day or two things got back to the old footing. I made what progress I could in the language, and in addition I pushed my explorations here and there. Either I missed some subtle point, or their language was excessively simple – almost exclusively composed of concrete substantives and verbs. There seemed to be few, if any, abstract terms, or little use of figurative language. Their sentences were usually simple and of two words, and I failed to convey or understand any but the simplest propositions. I determined to put the thought of my Time Machine and the mystery of the bronze doors under the sphinx as much as possible in a corner of memory, until my growing knowledge would lead me back to them in a natural way. Yet a certain feeling, you may understand, tethered me in a circle of a few miles round the point of my arrival.

'So far as I could see, all the world displayed the same exuberant richness as the Thames valley. From every hill I climbed I saw the same abundance of splendid buildings, endlessly varied in material and style, the same clustering thickets of evergreens, the same blossom-laden trees and tree-ferns. Here and there water shone like silver, and beyond, the land rose into blue undulating hills, and so faded into the serenity of the sky. A peculiar feature, which presently attracted my attention, was the presence of certain circular wells, several, as it seemed to me, of a very great depth. One lay by the path up the hill, which I had followed during my first walk. Like the others, it was rimmed with bronze, curiously wrought, and protected by a little cupola from the rain. Sitting by the side of these wells, and peering down into the shafted darkness, I could see no gleam of water, nor could I start any reflection with a lighted match. But in all of them I heard a certain sound: a thud – thud – thud, like the beating of some big engine; and I discovered, from the flaring of my matches, that a steady current of air set down the shafts. Further, I threw a scrap of paper into the throat of one, and, instead of fluttering slowly down, it was at once sucked swiftly out of sight.

'After a time, too, I came to connect these wells with tall towers standing here and there upon the slopes; for above them there was often just such a flicker in the air as one sees on a hot day above a sun-scorched beach. Putting things together, I reached a strong suggestion of an extensive system of subterranean ventilation, whose true import it was difficult to imagine. I was at first inclined to associate it with the sanitary apparatus of these people. It was an obvious conclusion, but it was absolutely wrong.

'And here I must admit that I learned very little of drains and bells and modes of conveyance, and the like conveniences, during my time in this real future. In some of these visions of Utopias and coming times which I have read, there is a vast amount of detail about building, and social arrangements, and so forth. But while such details are easy enough to obtain when the whole world is contained in one's imagination, they are altogether inaccessible to a real traveller amid such realities as I found here. Conceive the tale of London which a negro, fresh from Central Africa, would take back to his tribe! What would he know of railway companies, of social movements, of telephone and telegraph wires, of the Parcels Delivery Company, and postal orders and the like? Yet we, at least, should be willing enough to explain these things to him! And even of what he knew, how much could he make his untravelled friend either apprehend or believe? Then, think how narrow the gap between a negro and a white man of our own times, and how wide the interval between myself and these of the Golden Age! I was sensible of much which was unseen, and which contributed to my comfort; but save for a general impression of automatic organisation, I fear I can convey very little of the difference to your mind.

'In the matter of sepulture, for instance, I could see no signs of crematoria nor anything suggestive of tombs. But it occurred to me that, possibly, there might be cemeteries (or crematoria) somewhere beyond the range of my explorings. This, again, was a question I deliberately put to myself, and my curiosity was at first entirely defeated upon the point. The thing puzzled me, and I was led to make a further remark, which puzzled me still more: that aged and infirm among this people there were none.

'I must confess that my satisfaction with my first theories of an automatic civilization and a decadent humanity did not long endure. Yet I could think of no other. Let me put my difficulties. The several big palaces I had explored were mere living places, great dining-halls and sleeping apartments. I could find no machinery, no appliances of any kind. Yet these people were clothed in pleasant fabrics that must at times need renewal, and their sandals, though undecorated, were fairly complex specimens of metal-work. Somehow such things must be made. And the little people displayed no vestige of a creative tendency. There were no shops, no workshops, no sign of importations among them. They spent all their time in playing gently, in bathing in the river, in making love in a half-playful fashion, in eating fruit and sleeping. I could not see how things were kept going.

'Then, again, about the Time Machine: something, I knew not what, had taken it into the hollow pedestal of the White Sphinx. Why? For the life of me I could not imagine. Those waterless wells, too, those flickering pillars. I felt I lacked a clue. I felt – how shall I put it? Suppose you found an inscription, with sentences here and there in excellent plain English, and, inter-polated therewith, others made up of words, of letters even, absolutely unknown to you? Well, on the third day of my visit, that was how the world of Eight Hundred and Two Thousand Seven Hundred and One presented itself to me!

'That day, too, I made a friend – of a sort. It happened that, as I was watching some of the little people bathing in a shallow, one of them was seized with cramp and began drifting down-stream. The main current ran rather swiftly, but not too strongly for even a moderate swimmer. It will give you an idea, therefore, of the strange deficiency in these creatures, when I tell you that none made the slightest attempt to rescue the weakly crying little thing which was drowning before their eyes. When I realized this, I hurriedly slipped off my clothes, and, wading in at a point lower down, I caught the poor mite and drew her safe to land. A little rubbing of the limbs soon brought her round, and I had the satisfaction of seeing she was all right before I left her. I had got to such a low estimate of her kind that I did not expect any gratitude from her. In that, however, I was wrong.

'This happened in the morning. In the afternoon I met my little woman, as I believe it was, as I was returning towards my centre from an exploration, and she received me with cries of delight and presented me with a big garland of flowers – evidently made for me and me alone. The thing took my imagination. Very possibly I had been feeling desolate. At any rate I did my best to display my appreciation of the gift. We were soon seated together in a little stone arbour, engaged in conversation, chiefly of smiles. The creature's friendliness affected me exactly as a child's might have done. We passed each other flowers, and she kissed my hands. I did the same to hers. Then I tried talk, and found that her name was Weena, which, though I don't know what it meant, somehow seemed appropriate enough. That was the beginning of a queer friendship which lasted a week, and ended – as I will tell you!

'She was exactly like a child. She wanted to be with me always. She tried to follow me everywhere, and on my next journey out and about it went to my heart to tire her down, and leave her at last, exhausted and calling after me rather plaintively. But the problems of the world had to be mastered. I had not, I said to myself, come into the future to carry on a miniature flirtation. Yet her distress when I left her was very great, her expostulations at the parting were sometimes frantic, and I think, altogether, I had as much trouble as comfort from her devotion. Nevertheless she was, somehow, a very great comfort. I thought it was mere childish affection that made her cling to me. Until it was too late, I did not clearly know what I had inflicted upon her when I left her. Nor until it was too late did I clearly understand what she was to me. For, by merely seeming fond of me, and showing in her weak, futile way that she cared for me, the little doll of a creature presently gave my return to the neighbourhood of the White Sphinx almost the feeling of coming home; and I would watch for her tiny figure of white and gold so soon as I came over the hill.

'It was from her, too, that I learned that fear had not yet left the world. She was fearless enough in the daylight, and she had the oddest confidence in me; for once, in a foolish moment, I made threatening grimaces at her, and she simply laughed at them. But she dreaded the dark, dreaded shadows, dreaded black things. Darkness to her was the one thing dreadful. It was a singularly passionate emotion, and it set me thinking and observing. I discovered then, among other things, that these little people gathered into the great houses after dark, and slept in droves. To enter upon them without a light was to put them into a tumult of apprehension. I never found one out of doors, or one sleeping alone within doors, after dark. Yet I was still such a blockhead that I missed the lesson of that fear, and in spite of Weena's distress I insisted upon sleeping away from these slumbering multitudes.

'It troubled her greatly, but in the end her odd affection for me triumphed, and for five of the nights of our acquaintance, including the last night of all, she slept with her head pillowed on my arm. But my story slips away from me as I speak of her. It must have been the night before her rescue that I was awakened about dawn. I had been restless, dreaming most disagreeably that I was drowned, and that sea-anemones were feeling over my face with their soft palps. I woke with a start, and with an odd fancy that some greyish animal had just rushed out of the chamber. I tried to get to sleep again, but I felt restless and uncomfortable. It was that dim grey hour when things are just creeping out of darkness, when everything is colourless and clear cut, and yet unreal. I got up, and went down into the great hall, and so out upon the flagstones in front of the palace. I thought I would make a virtue of necessity, and see the sunrise.

'The moon was setting, and the dying moonlight and the first pallor of dawn were mingled in a ghastly half-light. The bushes were inky black, the ground a sombre grey, the sky colourless and cheerless. And up the hill I thought I could see ghosts. Three several times, as I scanned the slope, I saw white figures. Twice I fancied I saw a solitary white, ape-like creature running rather quickly up the hill, and once near the ruins I saw a leash of them carrying some dark body. They moved hastily. I did not see what became of them. It seemed that they vanished among the bushes. The dawn was still indistinct, you must understand. I was feeling that chill, uncertain, early-morning feeling you may have known. I doubted my eyes.

'As the eastern sky grew brighter, and the light of the day came on and its vivid colouring returned upon the world once more, I scanned the view keenly. But I saw no vestige of my white figures. There were mere creatures of the half-light. "They must have been ghosts," I said; "I wonder whence they dated." For a queer notion of Grant Allen's came into my head, and amused me. If each generation die and leave ghosts, he argued, the world at last will get overcrowded with them. On that theory they would have grown innumerable some Eight Hundred Thousand years hence, and it was no great wonder to see four at once. But the jest was unsatisfying, and I was thinking of these figures all the morning, until Weena's rescue drove them out of my head. I associated them in some indefinite way with the white animal I had startled in my first passionate search for the Time Machine. But Weena was a pleasant substitute. Yet all the same, they were soon destined to take far deadlier possession of my mind.

'I think I have said how much hotter than our own was the weather of this Golden Age. I cannot account for it. It may be that the sun was hotter, or the earth nearer the sun. It is usual to assume that the sun will go on cooling steadily in the future. But people, unfamiliar with such speculations as those of the younger Darwin, forget that the planets must ultimately fall back one by one into the parent body. As these catastrophes occur, the sun will blaze with renewed energy; and it may be that some inner planet had suffered this fate. Whatever the reason, the fact remains that the sun was very much hotter than we know it.

'Well, one very hot morning – my fourth, I think – as I was seeking shelter from the heat and glare in a colossal ruin near the great house where I slept and fed, there happened this strange thing: Clambering among these heaps of masonry, I found a narrow gallery, whose end and side windows were blocked by fallen masses of stone. By contrast with the brilliancy outside, it seemed at first impenetrably dark to me. I entered it groping, for the change from light to blackness made spots of colour swim before me. Suddenly I halted spellbound. A pair of eyes, luminous by reflection against the daylight without, was watching me out of the darkness.

'The old instinctive dread of wild beasts came upon me. I clenched my hands and steadfastly looked into the glaring eyeballs. I was afraid to turn. Then the thought of the absolute security in which humanity appeared to be living came to my mind. And then I remembered that strange terror of the dark. Overcoming my fear to some extent, I advanced a step and spoke. I will admit that my voice was harsh and ill-controlled. I put out my hand and touched something soft. At once the eyes darted sideways, and something white ran past me. I turned with my heart in my mouth, and saw a queer little ape-like figure, its head held down in a peculiar manner, running across the sunlit space behind me. It blundered against a block of granite, staggered aside, and in a moment was hidden in a black shadow beneath another pile of ruined masonry.

'My impression of it is, of course, imperfect; but I know it was a dull white, and had strange large greyish-red eyes; also that there was flaxen hair on its head and down its back. But, as I say, it went too fast for me to see distinctly. I cannot even say whether it ran on all-fours, or only with its forearms held very low. After an instant's pause I followed it into the second heap of ruins. I could not find it at first; but, after a time in the profound obscurity, I came upon one of those round well-like openings of which I have told you, half closed by a fallen pillar. A sudden thought came to me. Could this Thing have vanished down the shaft? I lit a match, and, looking down, I saw a small, white, moving creature, with large bright eyes which regarded me steadfastly as it retreated. It made me shudder. It was so like a human spider! It was clambering down the wall, and now I saw for the first time a number of metal foot and hand rests forming a kind of ladder down the shaft. Then the light burned my fingers and fell out of my hand, going out as it dropped, and when I had lit another the little monster had disappeared.

'I do not know how long I sat peering down that well. It was not for some time that I could succeed in persuading myself that the thing I had seen was human. But, gradually, the truth dawned on me: that Man had not remained one species, but had differentiated into two distinct animals: that my graceful children of the Upperworld were not the sole descendants of our generation, but that this bleached, obscene, nocturnal Thing, which had flashed before me, was also heir to all the ages.

'I thought of the flickering pillars and of my theory of an underground ventilation. I began to suspect their true import. And what, I wondered, was this Lemur doing in my scheme of a perfectly balanced organization? How was it related to the indolent serenity of the beautiful Upper-worlders? And what was hidden down there, at the foot of that shaft? I sat upon the edge of the well telling myself that, at any rate, there was nothing to fear, and that there I must descend for the solution of my difficulties. And withal I was absolutely afraid to go! As I hesitated, two of the beautiful Upperworld people came running in their amorous sport across the daylight into the shadow. The male pursued the female, flinging flowers at her as he ran.

'They seemed distressed to find me, my arm against the overturned pillar, peering down the well. Apparently it was considered bad form to remark these apertures; for when I pointed to this one, and tried to frame a question about it in their tongue, they were still more visibly distressed and turned away. But they were interested by my matches, and I struck some to amuse them. I tried them again about the well, and again I failed. So presently I left them, meaning to go back to

Weena, and see what I could get from her. But my mind was already in revolution; my guesses and impressions were slipping and sliding to a new adjustment. I had now a clue to the import of these wells, to the ventilating towers, to the mystery of the ghosts; to say nothing of a hint at the meaning of the bronze gates and the fate of the Time Machine! And very vaguely there came a suggestion towards the solution of the economic problem that had puzzled me.

'Here was the new view. Plainly, this second species of Man was subterranean. There were three circumstances in particular which made me think that its rare emergence above ground was the outcome of a long-continued underground habit. In the first place, there was the bleached look common in most animals that live largely in the dark – the white fish of the Kentucky caves, for instance. Then, those large eyes, with that capacity for reflecting light, are common features of nocturnal things – witness the owl and the cat. And last of all, that evident confusion in the sunshine, that hasty yet fumbling and awkward flight towards dark shadow, and that peculiar carriage of the head while in the light – all reinforced the theory of an extreme sensitiveness of the retina.

'Beneath my feet, then, the earth must be tunnelled enormously, and these tunnellings were the habitat of the new race. The presence of ventilating-shafts and wells along the hill slopes – everywhere, in fact, except along the river valley – showed how universal were its ramifications. What so natural, then, as to assume that it was in this artificial Underworld that such work as was necessary to the comfort of the daylight race was done? The notion was so plausible that I at once accepted it, and went on to assume the *how* of this splitting of the human species. I dare say you will anticipate the shape of my theory; though, for myself, I very soon felt that it fell far short of the truth.

'At first, proceeding from the problems of our own age, it seemed clear as daylight to me that the gradual widening of the present merely temporary and social difference between the Capitalist and the Labourer, was the key to the whole position. No doubt it will seem grotesque enough to you – and wildly incredible! – and yet even now there are existing circumstances to point that way. There is a tendency to utilize underground space for the less ornamental purposes of civilization; there is the Metropolitan Railway in London, for instance, there are new electric railways, there are subways, there are underground workrooms and restaurants, and they increase and multiply. Evidently, I thought, this tendency had increased till Industry had gradually lost its birthright in the sky. I mean that it had gone deeper and deeper into larger and ever larger underground factories, spending a still-increasing amount of its time therein, till, in the end – ! Even now, does not an East-end worker live in such artificial conditions as practically to be cut off from the natural surface of the earth?

'Again, the exclusive tendency of richer people – due, no doubt, to the increasing refinement of their education, and the widening gulf between them and the rude violence of the poor – is already leading to the closing, in their interest, of considerable portions of the surface of the land. About London, for instance, perhaps half the prettier country is shut in against intrusion. And this same widening gulf – which is due to the length and expense of the higher educational process and the increased facilities for and temptations towards refined habits on the part of the rich – will make that exchange between class and class, that promotion by intermarriage which at present retards the splitting of our species along lines of social stratification, less and less frequent. So, in the end, above ground you must have the Haves, pursuing pleasure and comfort and beauty, and below ground the Have-nots, the Workers getting continually adapted to the conditions of their labour. Once they were there, they would no doubt have to pay rent, and not a little of it, for the ventilation of their caverns; and if they refused, they would starve or be suffocated for arrears. Such of them as were so constituted as to be miserable and rebellious would die; and, in the end, the balance being permanent, the survivors would become as well adapted to the conditions of underground life, and as happy in their way, as the Upperworld people were to theirs. As it seemed to me, the refined beauty and the etiolated pallor followed naturally enough.

'The great triumph of Humanity I had dreamed of took a different shape in my mind. It had been no such triumph of moral education and general co-operation as I had imagined. Instead, I saw a real aristocracy, armed with a perfected science and working to a logical conclusion the industrial system of to-day. Its triumph had not been simply a triumph over Nature, but a triumph over Nature and the fellow-man. This, I must warn you, was my theory at the time. I had no convenient cicerone in the pattern of the Utopian books. My explanation may be absolutely wrong. I still think it is the most plausible one. But even on this supposition the balanced civilisation that was at last attained must have long since passed its zenith, and was now far fallen into decay. The too-perfect security of the Upper-worlders had led them to a slow movement of degeneration, to a general dwindling in size, strength, and intelligence. That I could see clearly enough already. What had happened to the Undergrounders I did not yet suspect; but from what I had seen of the Morlocks – that, by the by, was the name by which these creatures were called – I could imagine that the modification of the human type was even far more profound than among the "Eloi", the beautiful race that I already knew.

'Then came troublesome doubts. Why had the Morlocks taken my Time Machine? For I felt sure it was they who had taken it. Why, too, if the Eloi were masters, could they not restore the machine to me? And why were they so terribly afraid of the dark? I proceeded, as I have said, to question Weena about this Underworld, but here again I was disappointed. At first she would not understand my questions, and presently she refused to answer them. She shivered as though the topic was unendurable. And when I pressed her, perhaps a little harshly, she burst into tears. They were the only tears, except my own, I ever saw in that Golden Age. When I saw them I ceased abruptly to trouble about the Morlocks, and was only concerned in banishing these signs of her human inheritance from Weena's eyes. And very soon she was smiling and clapping her hands, while I solemnly burned a match.

6

'It may seem odd to you, but it was two days before I could follow up the new-found clue in what was manifestly the proper way. I felt a peculiar shrinking from those pallid bodies. They were just the half-bleached colour of the worms and things one sees preserved in spirit in a zoological museum. And they were filthily cold to the touch. Probably my shrinking was largely due to the sympathetic influence of the Eloi, whose disgust of the Morlocks I now began to appreciate.

'The next night I did not sleep well. Probably my health was a little disordered. I was oppressed with perplexity and doubt. Once or twice I had a feeling of intense fear for which I could perceive no definite reason. I remember creeping noiselessly into the great hall where the little people were sleeping in the moonlight – that night Weena was among them – and feeling reassured by their presence. It occurred to me even then, that in the course of a few days the moon must pass through its last quarter, and the nights grow dark, when the appearances of these unpleasant creatures from below, these whitened Lemurs, this new vermin that had replaced the old, might be more abundant. And on both these days I had the restless feeling of one who shirks an inevitable duty. I felt assured that the Time Machine was only to be recovered by boldly penetrating these underground mysteries. Yet I could not face the mystery. If only I had had a companion it would have been different. But I was so horribly alone, and even to clamber down into the darkness of the well appalled me. I don't know if you will understand my feeling, but I never felt quite safe at my back.

'It was this restlessness, this insecurity, perhaps, that drove me further and further afield in my exploring expeditions. Going to the south-westward towards the rising country that is now called Combe Wood, I observed far off, in the direction of nineteenth-century Banstead, a vast green structure, different in character from any I had hitherto seen. It was larger than the largest of the palaces or ruins I knew, and the façade had an Oriental look: the face of it having the lustre, as well as the pale-green tint, a kind of bluish-green, of a certain type of Chinese porcelain. This difference in aspect suggested a difference in use, and I was minded to push on and explore. But the day was growing late, and I had come upon the sight of the place after a long and tiring circuit; so I resolved to hold over the adventure for the following day, and I returned to the welcome and the caresses of little Weena. But next morning I perceived clearly enough that my curiosity regarding the Palace of Green Porcelain was a piece of self-deception, to enable me to shirk, by another day, an experience I dreaded. I resolved I would make the descent without further waste of time, and started out in the early morning towards a well near the ruins of granite and aluminium.

'Little Weena ran with me. She danced beside me to the well, but when she saw me lean over the mouth and look downward, she seemed strangely disconcerted. "Good-bye, little Weena," I said, kissing her; and then, putting her down, I began to feel over the parapet for the climbing hooks. Rather hastily, I may as well confess, for I feared my courage might leak away! At first she watched me in amazement. Then she gave a most piteous cry, and, running to me, she began to pull at me with her little hands. I think her opposition nerved me rather to proceed. I shook her off, perhaps a little roughly, and in another moment I was in the throat of the well. I saw her agonized face over the parapet, and smiled to reassure her. Then I had to look down at the unstable hooks to which I clung.

'I had to clamber down a shaft of perhaps two hundred yards. The descent was effected by means of metallic bars projecting from the sides of the well, and these being adapted to the needs of a creature much smaller and lighter than myself, I was speedily cramped and fatigued by the descent. And not simply fatigued! One of the bars bent suddenly under my weight, and almost swung me off into the blackness beneath. For a moment I hung by one hand, and after that experience I did not dare to rest again. Though my arms and back were presently acutely painful, I went on clambering down the sheer descent with as quick a motion as possible. Glancing upward, I saw the aperture, a small blue disk, in which a star was visible, while little Weena's head showed as a round black projection. The thudding sound of a machine below grew louder and more oppressive. Everything save that little disk above was profoundly dark, and when I looked up again Weena had disappeared.

'I was in an agony of discomfort. I had some thought of trying to go up the shaft again, and leave the Underworld alone. But even while I turned this over in my mind I continued to descend. At last, with intense relief, I saw dimly coming up, a foot to the right of me, a slender loophole in the wall. Swinging myself in, I found it was the aperture of a narrow horizontal tunnel in which I could lie down and rest. It was not too soon. My arms ached, my back was cramped, and I was trembling with the prolonged terror of a fall. Besides this, the unbroken darkness had had a distressing effect upon my eyes. The air was full of the throb and hum of machinery pumping air down the shaft.

'I do not know how long I lay. I was roused by a soft hand touching my face. Starting up in the darkness I snatched at my matches and, hastily striking one, I saw three stooping white creatures similar to the one I had seen above ground in the ruin, hastily retreating before the light. Living, as they did, in what appeared to me impenetrable darkness, their eyes were abnormally large and sensitive, just as are the pupils of the abysmal fishes, and they reflected the light in the same way. I have no doubt they could see me in that rayless obscurity, and they did not seem to have any fear of me apart from the light. But, so soon as I struck a match in order to see them, they fled incontinently, vanishing into dark gutters and tunnels, from which their eyes glared at me in the strangest fashion.

'I tried to call to them, but the language they had was apparently different from that of the Upperworld people; so that I was needs left to my own unaided efforts, and the thought of flight before exploration was even then in my mind. But I said to myself, "You are in for it now," and, feeling my way along the tunnel, I found the noise of machinery grow louder. Presently the walls fell away from me, and I came to a large open space, and, striking another match, saw that I had entered a vast arched cavern, which stretched into utter darkness beyond the range of my light. The view I had of it was as much as one could see in the burning of a match.

'Necessarily my memory is vague. Great shapes like big machines rose out of the dimness, and cast grotesque black shadows, in which dim spectral Morlocks sheltered from the glare. The place, by the bye, was very stuffy and oppressive, and the faint halitus of freshly shed blood was in the air. Some way down the central vista was a little table of white metal, laid with what seemed a meal. The Morlocks at any rate were carnivorous! Even at the time, I remember wondering what large animal could have survived to furnish the red joint I saw. It was all very indistinct: the heavy smell, the big unmeaning shapes, the obscene figures lurking in the shadows, and only waiting for the darkness to come at me again! Then the match burned down, and stung my fingers, and fell, a wriggling red spot in the blackness.

'I have thought since how particularly ill-equipped I was for such an experience. When I had started with the Time Machine, I had started with the absurd assumption that the men of the Future would certainly be infinitely ahead of ourselves in all their appliances. I had come without arms, without medicine, without anything to smoke – at times I missed tobacco frightfully! – even without enough matches. If only I had thought of a Kodak! I could have flashed that glimpse of the Underworld in a second, and examined it at leisure. But, as it was, I stood there with only the weapons and the powers that Nature had endowed me with – hands, feet, and teeth; these, and four safety-matches that still remained to me.

'I was afraid to push my way in among all this machinery in the dark, and it was only with my last glimpse of light I discovered that my store of matches had run low. It had never occurred to me until that moment that there was any need to economize them, and I had wasted almost half the box in astonishing the Upper-worlders, to whom fire was a novelty. Now, as I say, I had four left, and while I stood in the dark, a hand touched mine, lank fingers came feeling over my face, and I was sensible of a peculiar unpleasant odour. I fancied I heard the breathing of a crowd of those dreadful little beings about me. I felt the box of matches in my hand being gently disengaged, and other hands behind me plucking at my clothing. The sense of these unseen creatures examining me was indescribably unpleasant. The sudden realisation of my ignorance of their ways of thinking and doing came home to me very vividly in the darkness. I shouted at them as loudly as I could. They started away, and then I could feel them approaching me again. They clutched at me more boldly, whispering odd sounds to each other. I shivered violently, and shouted again – rather discordantly. This time they were not so seriously alarmed, and they made a queer laughing noise as they came back at me. I will confess I was horribly frightened. I determined to strike another match and escape under the protection of its glare. I did so, and eking out the flicker with a scrap of paper from my pocket, I made good my retreat to the narrow tunnel. But I had scarce entered this when my light was blown out, and in the blackness I could hear the Morlocks rustling like wind among leaves, and pattering like the rain, as they hurried after me.

'In a moment I was clutched by several hands, and there was no mistaking that they were trying to haul me back. I struck another light, and waved it in their dazzled faces. You can scarce imagine how nauseatingly inhuman they looked – those pale, chinless faces and great, lidless, pinkish-grey eyes! – as they stared in their blindness and bewilderment. But I did not stay to look, I promise you: I retreated again, and when my second match had ended, I struck my third. It had almost burned through when I reached the opening into the shaft. I lay down on the edge, for the throb of the great pump below made me giddy. Then I felt sideways for the projecting hooks, and, as I did so, my feet were grasped from behind, and I was violently tugged backward. I lit my last match ... and it incontinently went out. But I had my hand on the climbing bars now, and, kicking violently, I disengaged myself from the clutches of the Morlocks and was speedily clambering up the shaft, while they stayed peering and blinking up at me: all but one little wretch who followed me for some way, and well-nigh secured my boot as a trophy.

'That climb seemed interminable to me. With the last twenty or thirty feet of it a deadly nausea came upon me. I had the greatest difficulty in keeping my hold. The last few yards was a frightful struggle against this faintness. Several times my head swam, and I felt all the sensations of falling. At last, however, I got over the well-mouth somehow, and staggered out of the ruin into the blinding sunlight. I fell upon my face. Even the soil smelt sweet and clean. Then I remember Weena kissing my hands and ears, and the voices of others among the Eloi. Then, for a time, I was insensible.

7

'Now, indeed, I seemed in a worse case than before. Hitherto, except during my night's anguish at the loss of the Time Machine, I had felt a sustaining hope of ultimate escape, but that hope was staggered by these new discoveries. Hitherto I had merely thought myself impeded by the childish simplicity of the little people, and by some unknown forces which I had only to understand to overcome; but there was an altogether new element in the sickening quality of the Morlocks – a something inhuman and malign. Instinctively I loathed them. Before, I had felt as a man might feel who had fallen into a pit: my concern was with the pit and how to get out of it. Now I felt like a beast in a trap, whose enemy would come upon him soon.

'The enemy I dreaded may surprise you. It was the darkness of the new moon. Weena had put this into my head by some at first incomprehensible remarks about the Dark Nights. It was not now such a very difficult problem to guess what the coming Dark Nights might mean. The moon was on the wane: each night there was a longer interval of darkness. And I now understood to some slight degree at least the reason of the fear of the little Upperworld people for the dark. I wondered vaguely what foul villainy it might be that the Morlocks did under the new moon. I felt pretty sure now that my second hypothesis was all wrong. The Upperworld people might once have been the favoured aristocracy, and the Morlocks their mechanical ser- vants; but that had long since passed away. The two species that had resulted from the evolution of man were sliding down towards, or had already arrived at, an altogether new relation- ship. The Eloi, like the Carlovingian kings, had decayed to a mere beautiful futility. They still possessed the earth on suffer- ance: since the Morlocks, subterranean for innumerable gener- ations, had come at last to find the daylit surface intolerable. And the Morlocks made their garments, I inferred, and main- tained them in their habitual needs, perhaps through the survival

of an old habit of service. They did it as a standing horse paws
with his foot, or as a man enjoys killing animals in sport:
because ancient and departed necessities had impressed it on the
organism. But, clearly, the old order was already in part
reversed. The Nemesis of the delicate ones was creeping on
apace. Ages ago, thousands of generations ago, man had thrust
his brother man out of the ease and the sunshine. And now that
brother was coming back – changed! Already the Eloi had begun
to learn one old lesson anew. They were becoming reacquainted
with Fear. And suddenly there came into my head the memory
of the meat I had seen in the Underworld. It seemed odd how it
floated into my mind: not stirred up as it were by the current of
my meditations, but coming in almost like a question from
outside. I tried to recall the form of it. I had a vague sense
of something familiar, but I could not tell what it was at the
time.

'Still, however helpless the little people in the presence of their
mysterious Fear, I was differently constituted. I came out of this
age of ours, this ripe prime of the human race, when Fear does
not paralyze and mystery has lost its terrors. I at least would
defend myself. Without further delay I determined to make
myself arms and a fastness where I might sleep. With that refuge
as a base, I could face this strange world with some of that
confidence I had lost in realising to what creatures night by
night I lay exposed. I felt I could never sleep again until my bed
was secure from them. I shuddered with horror to think how
they must already have examined me.

'I wandered during the afternoon along the valley of the
Thames, but found nothing that commended itself to my mind
as inaccessible. All the buildings and trees seemed easily practic-
able to such dexterous climbers as the Morlocks, to judge by
their wells, must be. Then the tall pinnacles of the Palace of
Green Porcelain and the polished gleam of its walls came back
to my memory; and in the evening, taking Weena like a child
upon my shoulder, I went up the hills towards the south-west.
The distance, I had reckoned, was seven or eight miles, but it
must have been nearer eighteen. I had first seen the place on a
moist afternoon when distances are deceptively diminished. In
addition, the heel of one of my shoes was loose, and a nail was
working through the sole – they were comfortable old shoes I
wore about indoors – so that I was lame. And it was already

long past sunset when I came in sight of the palace, silhouetted black against the pale yellow of the sky.

'Weena had been hugely delighted when I began to carry her, but after a time she desired me to let her down, and ran along by the side of me, occasionally darting off on either hand to pick flowers to stick in my pockets. My pockets had always puzzled Weena, but at the last she had concluded that they were an eccentric kind of vase for floral decoration. At least she utilized them for that purpose. And that reminds me! In changing my jacket I found . . .'

The Time Traveller paused, put his hand into his pocket, and silently placed two withered flowers, not unlike very large white mallows, upon the little table. Then he resumed his narrative.

'As the hush of evening crept over the world and we proceeded over the hill crest towards Wimbledon, Weena grew tired and wanted to return to the house of grey stone. But I pointed out the distant pinnacles of the Palace of Green Porcelain to her, and contrived to make her understand that we were seeking a refuge there from her Fear. You know that great pause that comes upon things before the dusk? Even the breeze stops in the trees. To me there is always an air of expectation about that evening stillness. The sky was clear, remote, and empty save for a few horizontal bars far down in the sunset. Well, that night the expectation took the colour of my fears. In that darkling calm my senses seemed preternaturally sharpened. I fancied I could even feel the hollowness of the ground beneath my feet: could, indeed, almost see through it the Morlocks on their ant-hill going hither and thither and waiting for the dark. In my excitement I fancied that they would receive my invasion of their burrows as a declaration of war. And why had they taken my Time Machine?

'So we went on in the quiet, and the twilight deepened into night. The clear blue of the distance faded, and one star after another came out. The ground grew dim and the trees black. Weena's fears and her fatigue grew upon her. I took her in my arms and talked to her and caressed her. Then, as the darkness grew deeper, she put her arms round my neck, and, closing her eyes, tightly pressed her face against my shoulder. So we went down a long slope into a valley, and there in the dimness I almost walked into a little river. This I waded, and went up the opposite side of the valley, past a number of sleeping houses, and by a statue – a Faun, or some such figure, *minus* the head. Here too were acacias. So far I had seen nothing of the Morlocks, but it was yet early in the night, and the darker hours before the old moon rose were still to come.

'From the brow of the next hill I saw a thick wood spreading wide and black before me. I hesitated at this. I could see no end to it, either to the right or the left. Feeling tired – my feet in particular, were very sore – I carefully lowered Weena from my shoulder as I halted, and sat down upon the turf. I could no longer see the Palace of Green Porcelain, and I was in doubt of my direction. I looked into the thickness of the wood and thought of what it might hide. Under that dense tangle of branches one would be out of sight of the stars. Even were there no other lurking danger – a danger I did not care to let my imagination loose upon – there would still be all the roots to stumble over and the tree-boles to strike against.

'I was very tired, too, after the excitements of the day; so I decided that I would not face it, but would pass the night upon the open hill.

'Weena, I was glad to find, was fast asleep. I carefully wrapped her in my jacket, and sat down beside her to wait for the moonrise. The hillside was quiet and deserted, but from the black of the wood there came now and then a stir of living things. Above me shone the stars, for the night was very clear. I felt a certain sense of friendly comfort in their twinkling. All the old constellations had gone from the sky, however: that slow movement which is imperceptible in a hundred human lifetimes, had long since rearranged them in unfamiliar groupings. But the Milky Way, it seemed to me, was still the same tattered streamer of star-dust as of yore. Southward (as I judged it) was a very bright red star that was new to me; it was even more splendid than our own green Sirius. And amid all these scintillating points of light one bright planet shone kindly and steadily like the face of an old friend.

'Looking at these stars suddenly dwarfed my own troubles and all the gravities of terrestrial life. I thought of their unfathomable distance, and the slow inevitable drift of their movements out of the unknown past into the unknown future. I thought of the great precessional cycle that the pole of the earth describes. Only forty times had that silent revolution occurred during all the years that I had traversed. And during these few revolutions all the activity, all the traditions, the complex organizations, the nations, languages, literatures, aspirations, even the mere memory of Man as I knew him, had been swept out of existence. Instead were these frail creatures who had forgotten their high ancestry, and the white Things of which I went in terror. Then I thought of the Great Fear that was between the two species, and for the first time, with a sudden shiver, came the clear knowledge of what the meat I had seen might be. Yet it was too horrible! I looked at little Weena sleeping beside me, her face white and starlike under the stars, and forthwith dismissed the thought.

'Through that long night I held my mind off the Morlocks as well as I could, and whiled away the time by trying to fancy I could find signs of the old constellations in the new confusion. The sky kept very clear, except for a hazy cloud or so. No doubt I dozed at times. Then, as my vigil wore on, came a faintness in the eastward sky, like the reflection of some colourless fire, and the old moon rose, thin and peaked and white. And close behind, and overtaking it, and overflowing it, the dawn came, pale at first, and then growing pink and warm. No Morlocks had approached us. Indeed, I had seen none upon the hill that night. And in the confidence of renewed day it almost seemed to me that my fear had been unreasonable. I stood up and found my foot with the loose heel swollen at the ankle and painful under the heel; so I sat down again, took off my shoes, and flung them away.

'I awakened Weena, and we went down into the wood, now green and pleasant instead of black and forbidding. We found some fruit wherewith to break our fast. We soon met others of the dainty ones, laughing and dancing in the sunlight as though there was no such thing in nature as the night. And then I thought once more of the meat that I had seen. I felt assured now of what it was, and from the bottom of my heart I pitied this last feeble rill from the great flood of humanity. Clearly, at some time in the Long-Ago of human decay the Morlocks' food had run short. Possibly they had lived on rats and suchlike vermin. Even now man is far less discriminating and exclusive in his food than he was – far less than any monkey. His prejudice against human flesh is no deep-seated instinct. And so these inhuman sons of men – ! I tried to look at the thing in a scientific spirit. After all, they were less human and more remote than our cannibal ancestors of three or four thousand years ago. And the intelligence that would have made this state of things a torment had gone. Why should I trouble myself? These Eloi were mere fatted cattle, which the ant-like Morlocks preserved and preyed upon – probably saw to the breeding of. And there was Weena dancing at my side!

'Then I tried to preserve myself from the horror that was coming upon me, by regarding it as a rigorous punishment of human selfishness. Man had been content to live in ease and delight upon the labours of his fellow-man, had taken Necessity as his watchword and excuse, and in the fulness of time Necessity had come home to him. I even tried a Carlyle-like scorn of this wretched aristocracy in decay. But this attitude of mind was impossible. However great their intellectual degradation, the Eloi had kept too much of the human form not to claim my sympathy, and to make me perforce a sharer in their degradation and their Fear.

'I had at that time very vague ideas as to the course I should pursue. My first was to secure some safe place of refuge, and to make myself such arms of metal or stone as I could contrive. That necessity was immediate. In the next place, I hoped to procure some means of fire, so that I should have the weapon of a torch at hand, for nothing, I knew, would be more efficient against these Morlocks. Then I wanted to arrange some contrivance to break open the doors of bronze under the White Sphinx. I had in mind a battering-ram. I had a persuasion that if I could enter those doors and carry a blaze of light before me I should discover the Time Machine and escape. I could not imagine the Morlocks were strong enough to move it far away. Weena I had resolved to bring with me to our own time. And turning such schemes over in my mind I pursued our way towards the building which my fancy had chosen as our dwelling.

'I found the Palace of Green Porcelain, when we approached it about noon, deserted and falling into ruin. Only ragged vestiges of glass remained in its windows, and great sheets of the green facing had fallen away from the corroded metallic framework. It lay very high upon a turfy down, and looking north-eastward before I entered it, I was surprised to see a large estuary, or even creek, where I judged Wandsworth and Battersea must once have been. I thought then – though I never followed up the thought – of what might have happened, or might be happening, to the living things in the sea.

'The material of the Palace proved on examination to be indeed porcelain, and along the face of it I saw an inscription in some unknown character. I thought, rather foolishly, that Weena might help me to interpret this, but I only learned that the bare idea of writing had never entered her head. She always seemed to me, I fancy, more human than she was, perhaps because her affection was so human.

'Within the big valves of the door – which were open and broken – we found, instead of the customary hall, a long gallery lit by many side windows. At the first glance I was reminded of a museum. The tiled floor was thick with dust, and a remarkable array of miscellaneous objects was shrouded in the same grey covering. Then I perceived, standing strange and gaunt in the centre of the hall, what was clearly the lower part of a huge skeleton. I recognized by the oblique feet that it was some extinct creature after the fashion of the Megatherium. The skull and the upper bones lay beside it in the thick dust, and in one place, where rain-water had dropped through a leak in the roof, the thing itself had been worn away. Further in the gallery was the huge skeleton barrel of a Brontosaurus. My museum hypothesis was confirmed. Going towards the side I found what appeared to be sloping shelves, and, clearing away the thick dust, I found the old familiar glass cases of our own time. But they must have been air-tight to judge from the fair preservation of some of their contents.

'Clearly we stood among the ruins of some latter-day South Kensington! Here, apparently, was the Palæontological Section, and a very splendid array of fossils it must have been, though the inevitable process of decay that had been staved off for a time, and had, through the extinction of bacteria and fungi, lost ninety-nine hundredths of its force, was, nevertheless, with extreme sureness if with extreme slowness at work again upon all its treasures. Here and there I found traces of the little people in the shape of rare fossils broken to pieces or threaded in strings upon reeds. And the cases had in some instances been bodily removed – by the Morlocks as I judged. The place was very silent. The thick dust deadened our footsteps. Weena, who had been rolling a sea-urchin down the sloping glass of a case, presently came, as I stared about me, and very quietly took my hand and stood beside me.

'And at first I was so much surprised by this ancient monument of an intellectual age, that I gave no thought to the possibilities it presented. Even my preoccupation about the Time Machine receded a little from my mind.

'To judge from the size of the place, this Palace of Green Porcelain had a great deal more in it than a Gallery of Palæontology; possibly historical galleries; it might be, even a library! To me, at least in my present circumstances, these would be vastly more interesting than this spectacle of old-time geology in decay. Exploring, I found another short gallery running transversely to the first. This appeared to be devoted to minerals, and the sight of a block of sulphur set my mind running on gunpowder. But I could find no saltpetre; indeed, no nitrates of any kind. Doubtless they had deliquesced ages ago. Yet the sulphur hung in my mind, and set up a train of thinking. As for the rest of the contents of that gallery, though on whole they were the best preserved of all I saw, I had little interest. I am no specialist in mineralogy, and I went on down a very ruinous aisle running parallel to the first hall I had entered. Apparently this section had been devoted to natural history, but everything had long since passed out of recognition. A few shrivelled and blackened vestiges of what had once been stuffed animals, desiccated mummies in jars that had once held spirit, a brown dust of departed plants; that was all! I was sorry for that, because I should have been glad to trace the patient readjustments by which the conquest of animated nature had been attained. Then we came to a gallery of simply colossal proportions, but singularly ill-lit, the floor of it running downward at a slight angle from the end at which I entered. At intervals white globes hung from the ceiling – many of them cracked and smashed – which suggested that originally the place had been artificially lit. Here I was more in my element, for rising on either side of me were the huge bulks of big machines, all greatly corroded and many broken down, but some still fairly complete. You know I have a certain weakness for mechanism, and I was inclined to linger among these; the more so as for the most part they had the interest of puzzles, and I could make only the vaguest guesses at what they were for. I fancied that if I could solve their puzzles I should find myself in possession of powers that might be of use against the Morlocks.

'Suddenly Weena came very close to my side. So suddenly that she startled me. Had it not been for her I do not think I should have noticed that the floor of the gallery sloped at all.* The end I had come in at was quite above ground, and was lit by rare slit-like windows. As you went down the length, the ground came up against these windows, until at last there was a pit like the "area" of a London house before each, and only a narrow line of daylight at the top. I went slowly along, puzzling about the machines, and had been too intent upon them to notice the gradual diminution of the light, until Weena's increasing apprehensions drew my attention. Then I saw that the gallery ran down at last into a thick darkness. I hesitated, and then, as I looked round me, I saw that the dust was less abundant and its surface less even. Further away towards the dimness, it appeared to be broken by a number of small narrow footprints. My sense of the immediate presence of the Morlocks revived at that. I felt that I was wasting my time in this academic examination of machinery. I called to mind that it was already far advanced in the afternoon, and that I had still no weapon, no refuge, and no means of making a fire. And then down in the remote blackness of the gallery I heard a peculiar pattering, and the same odd noises I had heard down the well.

* It may be, of course, that the floor did not slope, but that the museum was built into the side of a hill. – ED.

'I took Weena's hand. Then, struck with a sudden idea, I left her and turned to a machine from which projected a lever not unlike those in a signal-box. Clambering upon the stand, and grasping this lever in my hands, I put all my weight upon it sideways. Suddenly Weena, deserted in the central aisle, began to whimper. I had judged the strength of the lever pretty correctly, for it snapped after a minute's strain, and I rejoined her with a mace in my hand more than sufficient, I judged, for any Morlock skull I might encounter. And I longed very much to kill a Morlock or so. Very inhuman, you may think, to want to go killing one's own descendants! But it was impossible, somehow, to feel any humanity in the things. Only my disinclination to leave Weena, and a persuasion that if I began to slake my thirst for murder my Time Machine might suffer, restrained me from going straight down the gallery and killing the brutes I heard.

'Well, mace in one hand and Weena in the other, I went out of that gallery and into another and still larger one, which at the first glance reminded me of a military chapel hung with tattered flags. The brown and charred rags that hung from the sides of it, I presently recognized as the decaying vestiges of books. They had long since dropped to pieces, and every semblance of print had left them. But here and there were warped boards and cracked metallic clasps that told the tale well enough. Had I been a literary man I might, perhaps, have moralised upon the futility of all ambition. But as it was, the thing that struck me with keenest force was the enormous waste of labour to which this sombre wilderness of rotting paper testified. At the time I will confess that I thought chiefly of the *Philosophical Transactions* and my own seventeen papers upon physical optics.

'Then, going up a broad staircase, we came to what may once have been a gallery of technical chemistry. And here I had not a little hope of useful discoveries. Except at one end where the roof had collapsed, this gallery was well preserved. I went eagerly to every unbroken case. And at last, in one of the really airtight cases, I found a box of matches. Very eagerly I tried them. They were perfectly good. They were not even damp. I turned to Weena. "Dance," I cried to her in her own tongue. For now I had a weapon indeed against the horrible creatures we feared. And so, in that derelict museum, upon the thick soft carpeting of dust, to Weena's huge delight, I solemnly performed a kind of composite dance, whistling *The Land of the Leal* as cheerfully as I could. In part it was a modest *cancan*, in part a step-dance, in part a skirt-dance (so far as my tail-coat permitted), and in part original. For I am naturally inventive, as you know.

'Now, I still think that for this box of matches to have escaped the wear of time for immemorial years was a most strange, as for me it was a most fortunate thing. Yet, oddly enough, I found a far unlikelier substance, and that was camphor. I found it in a sealed jar, that by chance, I suppose, had been really hermetically sealed. I fancied at first that it was paraffin wax, and smashed the glass accordingly. But the odour of camphor was unmistakable. In the universal decay this volatile substance had chanced to survive, perhaps through many thousands of centuries. It reminded me of a sepia painting I had once seen done from the ink of a fossil Belemnite that must have perished and become fossilized millions of years ago. I was about to throw it away, but I remembered that it was inflammable and burned with a good bright flame – was, in fact, an excellent candle – and I put it in my pocket. I found no explosives, however, nor any means of breaking down the bronze doors. As yet my iron crowbar was the most helpful thing I had chanced upon. Nevertheless I left that gallery greatly elated.

'I cannot tell you all the story of that long afternoon. It would require a great effort of memory to recall my explorations in at all the proper order. I remember a long gallery of rusting stands of arms, and how I hesitated between my crowbar and a hatchet or a sword. I could not carry both, however, and my bar of iron promised best against the bronze gates. There were numbers of guns, pistols, and rifles. The most were masses of rust, but many were of some new metal, and still fairly sound. But any cartridges or powder there may once have been had rotted into dust. One corner I saw was charred and shattered; perhaps, I thought by an explosion among the specimens. In another place was a vast array of idols – Polynesian, Mexican, Grecian, Phœnician, every country on earth I should think. And here, yielding to an irresistible impulse, I wrote my name upon the nose of a steatite monster from South America that particularly took my fancy.

'As the evening drew on, my interest waned. I went through gallery after gallery, dusty, silent, often ruinous, the exhibits sometimes mere heaps of rust and lignite, sometimes fresher. In one place I suddenly found myself near the model of a tin-mine, and then by the merest accident I discovered, in an airtight case, two dynamite cartridges! I shouted "Eureka" and smashed the case with joy. Then came a doubt. I hesitated. Then, selecting a little side gallery, I made my essay. I never felt such a disappointment as I did in waiting five, ten, fifteen minutes for an explosion that never came. Of course the things were dummies, as I might have guessed from their presence. I really believe that, had they not been so, I should have rushed off incontinently and blown Sphinx, bronze doors, and (as it proved) my chances of finding the Time Machine, all together into non-existence.

'It was after that, I think, that we came to a little open court within the palace. It was turfed, and had three fruit-trees. So we rested and refreshed ourselves. Towards sunset I began to consider our position. Night was creeping upon us, and my inaccessible hiding-place had still to be found. But that troubled me very little now. I had in my possession a thing that was, perhaps, the best of all defences against the Morlocks – I had matches! I had the camphor in my pocket, too, if a blaze were needed. It seemed to me that the best thing we could do would be to pass the night in the open, protected by a fire. In the morning there was the getting of the Time Machine. Towards that, as yet, I had only my iron mace. But now, with my growing knowledge, I felt very differently towards those bronze doors. Up to this, I had refrained from forcing them, largely because of the mystery on the other side. They had never impressed me as being very strong, and I hoped to find my bar of iron not altogether inadequate for the work.

'We emerged from the palace while the sun was still in part above the horizon. I was determined to reach the White Sphinx early the next morning, and ere the dusk I purposed pushing through the woods that had stopped me on the previous journey. My plan was to go as far as possible that night, and then, building a fire, to sleep in the protection of its glare. Accordingly, as we went along I gathered any sticks or dried grass I saw, and presently had my arms full of such litter. Thus loaded, our progress was slower than I had anticipated, and besides Weena was tired. And I began to suffer from sleepiness too; so that it was full night before we reached the wood. Upon the shrubby hill of its edge Weena would have stopped, fearing the darkness before us; but a singular sense of impending calamity, that should indeed have served me as a warning, drove me onward. I had been without sleep for a night and two days, and I was feverish and irritable. I felt sleep coming upon me, and the Morlocks with it.

'While we hesitated, among the black bushes behind us, and dim against their blackness, I saw three crouching figures. There was scrub and long grass all about us, and I did not feel safe from their insidious approach. The forest, I calculated, was rather less than a mile across. If we could get through it to the bare hill-side, there, as it seemed to me, was an altogether safer resting-place; I thought that with my matches and my camphor I could contrive to keep my path illuminated through the woods. Yet it was evident that if I was to flourish matches with my hands I should have to abandon my firewood; so, rather reluctantly, I put it down. And then it came into my head that I would amaze our friends behind by lighting it. I was to discover the atrocious folly of this proceeding, but it came to my mind as an ingenious move for covering our retreat.

'I don't know if you have ever thought what a rare thing flame must be in the absence of man and in a temperate climate.

The sun's heat is rarely strong enough to burn, even when it is focused by dewdrops, as is sometimes the case in more tropical districts. Lightning may blast and blacken, but it rarely gives rise to widespread fire. Decaying vegetation may occasionally smoulder with the heat of its fermentation, but this rarely results in flame. In this decadence, too, the art of fire-making had been forgotten on the earth. The red tongues that went licking up my heap of wood were an altogether new and strange thing to Weena.

'She wanted to run to it and play with it. I believe she would have cast herself into it had I not restrained her. But I caught her up, and, in spite of her struggles, plunged boldly before me into the wood. For a little way the glare of my fire lit the path. Looking back presently, I could see, through the crowded stems, that from my heap of sticks the blaze had spread to some bushes adjacent, and a curved line of fire was creeping up the grass of the hill. I laughed at that, and turned again to the dark trees before me. It was very black, and Weena clung to me convulsively, but there was still, as my eyes grew accustomed to the darkness, sufficient light for me to avoid the stems. Overhead it was simply black, except where a gap of remote blue sky shone down upon us here and there. I struck none of my matches because I had no hand free. Upon my left arm I carried my little one, in my right hand I had my iron bar.

'For some way I heard nothing but the crackling twigs under my feet, the faint rustle of the breeze above, and my own breathing and the throb of the blood-vessels in my ears. Then I seemed to know of a pattering about me. I pushed on grimly. The pattering grew more distinct, and then I caught the same queer sounds and voices I had heard in the Underworld. There were evidently several of the Morlocks, and they were closing in upon me. Indeed, in another minute I felt a tug at my coat, then something at my arm. And Weena shivered violently, and became quite still.

'It was time for a match. But to get one I must put her down. I did so, and, as I fumbled with my pocket, a struggle began in the darkness about my knees, perfectly silent on her part and with the same peculiar cooing sounds from the Morlocks. Soft little hands, too, were creeping over my coat and back, touching even my neck. Then the match scratched and fizzed. I held it flaring, and saw the white backs of the Morlocks in flight amid the trees. I hastily took a lump of camphor from my pocket, and prepared to light it as soon as the match should wane. Then I looked at Weena. She was lying clutching my feet and quite motionless, with her face to the ground. With a sudden fright I stooped to her. She seemed scarcely to breathe. I lit the block of camphor and flung it to the ground, and as it spit and flared up and drove back the Morlocks and the shadows, I knelt down and lifted her. The wood behind seemed full of the stir and murmur of a great company!

'She seemed to have fainted. I put her carefully upon my shoulder and rose to push on, and then there came a horrible realization. In manoeuvring with my matches and Weena, I had turned myself about several times, and now I had not the faintest idea in what direction lay my path. For all I knew, I might be facing back towards the Palace of Green Porcelain. I found myself in a cold sweat. I had to think rapidly what to do. I determined to build a fire and encamp where we were. I put Weena, still motionless, down upon a turfy bole, and very hastily, as my first lump of camphor waned, I began collecting sticks and leaves. Here and there out of the darkness round me the Morlocks' eyes shone like carbuncles.

'The camphor flickered and went out. I lit a match, and as I did so, two white forms that had been approaching Weena dashed hastily away. One was so blinded by the light that he came straight for me and I felt his bones grind under the blow of my fist. He gave a whoop of dismay, staggered a little way, and fell down. I lit another piece of camphor, and went on gathering my bonfire. Presently I noticed how dry was some of the foliage above me, for since my arrival on the Time Machine, a matter of a week, no rain had fallen. So, instead of casting about among the trees for fallen twigs, I began leaping up and dragging down branches. Very soon I had a choking smoky fire of green wood and dry sticks, and could economize my camphor. Then I turned to where Weena lay beside my iron mace. I tried what I could to revive her, but she lay like one dead. I could not even satisfy myself whether or not she breathed.

'Now, the smoke of the fire beat over towards me, and it must have made me heavy of a sudden. Moreover, the vapour of camphor was in the air. My fire would not need replenishing for an hour or so. I felt very weary after my exertion, and sat down. The wood, too, was full of a slumbrous murmur that I did not understand. I seemed just to nod and open my eyes. But all was dark, and the Morlocks had their hands upon me. Flinging off their clinging fingers I hastily felt in my pocket for the match-box, and – it had gone! Then they gripped and closed with me again. In a moment I knew what had happened. I had slept, and my fire had gone out, and the bitterness of death came over my soul. The forest seemed full of the smell of burning wood. I was caught by the neck, by the hair, by the arms, and pulled down. It was indescribably horrible in the darkness to feel all these soft creatures heaped upon me. I felt as if I was in a monstrous spider's web. I was overpowered, and went down. I felt little teeth nipping at my neck. I rolled over, and as I did so my hand came against my iron lever. It gave me strength. I struggled up, shaking the human rats from me, and, holding the bar short, I thrust where I judged their faces might be. I could feel the succulent giving of flesh and bone under my blows, and for a moment I was free.

'The strange exultation that so often seems to accompany hard fighting came upon me. I knew that both I and Weena were lost, but I determined to make the Morlocks pay for their meat. I stood with my back to a tree, swinging the iron bar before me. The whole wood was full of the stir and cries of them. A minute passed. Their voices seemed to rise to a higher pitch of excitement, and their movements grew faster. Yet none came within reach. I stood glaring at the blackness. Then suddenly came hope. What if the Morlocks were afraid? And close on the heels of that came a strange thing. The darkness seemed to grow luminous. Very dimly I began to see the Morlocks about me – three battered at my feet – and then I recognized, with incredulous surprise, that the others were running, in an incessant stream, as it seemed, from behind me, and away through the wood in front. And their backs seemed no longer white, but reddish. As I stood agape, I saw a little red spark go drifting across a gap of starlight between the branches, and vanish. And at that I understood the smell of burning wood, the slumbrous murmur that was growing now into a gusty roar, the red glow, and the Morlocks' flight.

'Stepping out from behind my tree and looking back, I saw, through the black pillars of the nearer trees, the flames of the burning forest. It was my first fire coming after me. With that I looked for Weena, but she was gone. The hissing and crackling behind me, the explosive thud as each fresh tree burst into flame, left little time for reflection. My iron bar still gripped, I followed in the Morlocks' path. It was a close race. Once the flames crept forward so swiftly on my right as I ran that I was outflanked and had to strike off to the left. But at last I emerged upon a small open space, and as I did so, a Morlock came blundering towards me, and past me, and went on straight into the fire!

'And now I was to see the most weird and horrible thing, I think, of all that I beheld in that future age. This whole space was as bright as day with the reflection of the fire. In the centre was a hillock or tumulus, surmounted by a scorched hawthorn. Beyond this was another arm of the burning forest, with yellow tongues already writhing from it, completely encircling the space with a fence of fire. Upon the hill-side were some thirty or forty Morlocks, dazzled by the light and heat, and blundering hither and thither against each other in their bewilderment. At first I did not realize their blindness, and struck furiously at them with my bar, in a frenzy of fear, as they approached me, killing one and crippling several more. But when I had watched the gestures of one of them groping under the hawthorn against the red sky, and heard their moans, I was assured of their absolute helplessness and misery in the glare, and I struck no more of them.

'Yet every now and then one would come straight towards me, setting loose a quivering horror that made me quick to elude him. At one time the flames died down somewhat, and I feared the foul creatures would presently be able to see me. I was even thinking of beginning the fight by killing some of them before this should happen; but the fire burst out again brightly, and I stayed my hand. I walked about the hill among them and avoided them, looking for some trace of Weena. But Weena was gone.

'At last I sat down on the summit of the hillock, and watched this strange incredible company of blind things groping to and fro, and making uncanny noises to each other, as the glare of the fire beat on them. The coiling uprush of smoke streamed across the sky, and through the rare tatters of that red canopy, remote as though they belonged to another universe, shone the little stars. Two or three Morlocks came blundering into me, and I drove them off with blows of my fists, trembling as I did so.

'For the most part of that night I was persuaded it was a

nightmare. I bit myself and screamed in a passionate desire to awake. I beat the ground with my hands, and got up and sat down again, and wandered here and there, and again sat down. Then I would fall to rubbing my eyes and calling upon God to let me awake. Thrice I saw Morlocks put their heads down in a kind of agony and rush into the flames. But, at last, above the subsiding red of the fire, above the streaming masses of black smoke and the whitening and blackening tree stumps, and the diminishing numbers of these dim creatures, came the white light of the day.

'I searched again for traces of Weena, but there were none. It was plain that they had left her poor little body in the forest. I cannot describe how it relieved me to think that it had escaped the awful fate to which it seemed destined. As I thought of that, I was almost moved to begin a massacre of the helpless abominations about me, but I contained myself. The hillock, as I have said, was a kind of island in the forest. From its summit I could now make out through a haze of smoke the Palace of Green Porcelain, and from that I could get my bearings for the White Sphinx. And so, leaving the remnant of these damned souls going hither and thither and moaning, as the day grew clearer, I tied some grass about my feet and limped on across smoking ashes and among black stems, that still pulsated internally with fire, towards the hiding-place of the Time Machine. I walked slowly, for I was almost exhausted, as well as lame, and I felt the intensest wretchedness for the horrible death of little Weena. It seemed an overwhelming calamity. Now, in this old familiar room, it is more like the sorrow of a dream than an actual loss. But that morning it left me absolutely lonely again – terribly alone. I began to think of this house of mine, of this fireside, of some of you, and with such thoughts came a longing that was pain.

'But, as I walked over the smoking ashes under the bright morning sky, I made a discovery. In my trouser pocket were still some loose matches. The box must have leaked before it was lost.

10

'About eight or nine in the morning I came to the same seat of yellow metal from which I had viewed the world upon the evening of my arrival. I thought of my hasty conclusions upon that evening and could not refrain from laughing bitterly at my confidence. Here was the same beautiful scene, the same abundant foliage, the same splendid palaces and magnificent ruins, the same silver river running between its fertile banks. The gay robes of the beautiful people moved hither and thither among the trees. Some were bathing in exactly the place where I had saved Weena, and that suddenly gave me a keen stab of pain. And like blots upon the landscape rose the cupolas above the ways to the Underworld. I understood now what all the beauty of the Upperworld people covered. Very pleasant was their day, as pleasant as the day of the cattle in the field. Like the cattle, they knew of no enemies and provided against no needs. And their end was the same.

'I grieved to think how brief the dream of the human intellect had been. It had committed suicide. It had set itself steadfastly towards comfort and ease, a balanced society with security and permanency as its watchword, it had attained its hopes – to come to this at last. Once, life and property must have reached almost absolute safety. The rich had been assured of his wealth and comfort, the toiler assured of his life and work. No doubt in that perfect world there had been no unemployed problem, no social question left unsolved. And a great quiet had followed.

'It is a law of nature we overlook, that intellectual versatility is the compensation for change, danger, and trouble. An animal perfectly in harmony with its environment is a perfect mechanism. Nature never appeals to intelligence until habit and instinct are useless. There is no intelligence where there is no change and no need of change. Only those animals partake of intelligence that have to meet a huge variety of needs and dangers.

'So, as I see it, the Upperworld man had drifted towards his feeble prettiness, and the Underworld to mere mechanical industry. But that perfect state had lacked one thing even for mechanical perfection – absolute permanency. Apparently as time went on, the feeding of the Underworld, however it was effected, had become disjointed. Mother Necessity, who had been staved off for a few thousand years, came back again, and she began below. The Underworld being in contact with machinery, which, however perfect, still needs some little thought outside habit, had probably retained perforce rather more initiative, if less of every other human character, than the upper. And when other meat failed them, they turned to what old habit had hitherto forbidden. So I say I saw it in my last view of the world of Eight Hundred and Two Thousand Seven Hundred and One. It may be as wrong an explanation as mortal wit could invent. It is how the thing shaped itself to me, and as that I give it to you.

'After the fatigues, excitements, and terrors of the past days, and in spite of my grief, this seat and the tranquil view and the warm sunlight were very pleasant. I was very tired and sleepy, and soon my theorizing passed into dozing. Catching myself at that, I took my own hint, and spreading myself out upon the turf I had a long and refreshing sleep.

'I awoke a little before sunsetting. I now felt safe against being caught napping by the Morlocks, and, stretching myself, I came on down the hill towards the White Sphinx. I had my crowbar in one hand, and the other hand played with the matches in my pocket.

'And now came the most unexpected thing. As I approached the pedestal of the sphinx I found the bronze valves were open. They had slid down into grooves.

'At that I stopped short before them, hesitating to enter.

'Within was a small apartment, and on a raised place in the corner of this was the Time Machine. I had the small levers in my pocket. So here, after all my elaborate preparations for the siege of the White Sphinx, was a meek surrender. I threw my iron bar away, almost sorry not to use it.

'A sudden thought came into my head as I stooped towards the portal. For once, at least, I grasped the mental operations of the Morlocks. Suppressing a strong inclination to laugh, I stepped through the bronze frame and up to the Time Machine. I was surprised to find it had been carefully oiled and cleaned. I have suspected since that the Morlocks had even partially taken it to pieces while trying in their dim way to grasp its purpose.

'Now as I stood and examined it, finding a pleasure in the mere touch of the contrivance, the thing I had expected happened. The bronze panels suddenly slid up and struck the frame with a clang. I was in the dark – trapped. So the Morlocks thought. At that I chuckled gleefully.

'I could already hear their murmuring laughter as they came towards me. Very calmly I tried to strike the match. I had only to fix on the levers and depart then like a ghost. But I had overlooked one little thing. The matches were of that abominable kind that light only on the box.

'You may imagine how all my calm vanished. The little brutes were close upon me. One touched me. I made a sweeping blow in the dark at them with the levers, and began to scramble into the saddle of the machine. Then came one hand upon me and then another. Then I had simply to fight against their persistent fingers for my levers, and at the same time feel for the studs over which these fitted. One, indeed, they almost got away from me. As it slipped from my hand, I had to butt in the dark with my head – I could hear the Morlock's skull ring – to recover it. It was a nearer thing than the fight in the forest, I think, this last scramble.

'But at last the lever was fixed and pulled over. The clinging hands slipped from me. The darkness presently fell from my eyes. I found myself in the same grey light and tumult I have already described.

11

'I have already told you of the sickness and confusion that comes with time travelling. And this time I was not seated properly in the saddle, but sideways and in an unstable fashion. For an indefinite time I clung to the machine as it swayed and vibrated, quite unheeding how I went, and when I brought myself to look at the dials again I was amazed to find where I had arrived. One dial records days, another thousands of days, another millions of days, and another thousands of millions. Now, instead of reversing the levers, I had pulled them over so as to go forward with them, and when I came to look at these indicators I found that the thousands hand was sweeping round as fast as the seconds hand of a watch – into futurity.

'As I drove on, a peculiar change crept over the appearance of things. The palpitating greyness grew darker; then – though I was still travelling with prodigious velocity – the blinking succession of day and night, which was usually indicative of a slower pace, returned, and grew more and more marked. This puzzled me very much at first. The alternations of night and day grew slower and slower, and so did the passage of the sun across the sky, until they seemed to stretch through centuries. At last a steady twilight brooded over the earth, a twilight only broken now and then when a comet glared across the darkling sky. The band of light that had indicated the sun had long since disappeared; for the sun had ceased to set – it simply rose and fell in the west, and grew ever broader and more red. All trace of the moon had vanished. The circling of the stars, growing slower and slower, had given place to creeping points of light. At last, some time before I stopped, the sun, red and very large, halted motionless upon the horizon, a vast dome glowing with a dull heat, and now and then suffering a momentary extinction. At one time it had for a little while glowed more brilliantly again, but it speedily reverted to its sullen red heat. I perceived by this slowing down of its rising and setting that the work of the tidal drag was done. The earth had come to rest with one face to the sun, even as in our own time the moon faces the earth. Very cautiously, for I remembered my former headlong fall, I began to reverse my motion. Slower and slower went the circling hands until the thousands one seemed motionless and the daily one was no longer a mere mist upon its scale. Still slower, until the dim outlines of a desolate beach grew visible.

'I stopped very gently and sat upon the Time Machine, looking round. The sky was no longer blue. North-eastward it was inky black, and out of the blackness shone brightly and steadily the pale white stars. Overhead it was a deep Indian red and starless, and south-eastward it grew brighter to a glowing scarlet where, cut by the horizon, lay the huge hull of the sun, red and motionless. The rocks about me were of a harsh reddish colour, and all the trace of life that I could see at first was the intensely green vegetation that covered every projecting point on their south-eastern face. It was the same rich green that one sees on forest moss or on the lichen in caves: plants which like these grow in a perpetual twilight.

'The machine was standing on a sloping beach. The sea stretched away to the south-west, to rise into a sharp bright horizon against the wan sky. There were no breakers and no waves, for not a breath of wind was stirring. Only a slight oily swell rose and fell like a gentle breathing, and showed that the eternal sea was still moving and living. And along the margin where the water sometimes broke was a thick incrustation of salt – pink under the lurid sky. There was a sense of oppression in my head, and I noticed that I was breathing very fast. The sensation reminded me of my only experience of mountaineering, and from that I judged the air to be more rarefied than it is now.

'Far away up the desolate slope I heard a harsh scream, and saw a thing like a huge white butterfly go slanting and fluttering up into the sky and, circling, disappear over some low hillocks beyond. The sound of its voice was so dismal that I shivered and seated myself more firmly upon the machine. Looking round me again, I saw that, quite near, what I had taken to be a reddish mass of rock was moving slowly towards me. Then I saw the thing was really a monstrous crab-like creature. Can you imagine a crab as large as yonder table, with its many legs moving slowly and uncertainly, its big claws swaying, its long antennæ, like carters' whips, waving and feeling, and its stalked eyes gleaming at you on either side of its metallic front? Its back was corrugated and ornamented with ungainly bosses, and a greenish incrustation blotched it here and there. I could see the many palps of its complicated mouth flickering and feeling as it moved.

'As I stared at this sinister apparition crawling towards me, I felt a tickling on my cheek as though a fly had lighted there. I tried to brush it away with my hand, but in a moment it returned, and almost immediately came another by my ear. I struck at this and caught something threadlike. It was drawn swiftly out of my hand. With a frightful qualm, I turned, and saw that I had grasped the antenna of another monster crab that stood just behind me. Its evil eyes were wriggling on their stalks, its mouth was all alive with appetite, and its vast ungainly claws, smeared with an algal slime, were descending upon me. In a moment my hand was on the lever, and I had placed a month between myself and these monsters. But I was still on the same beach, and I saw them distinctly now as soon as I stopped. Dozens of them seemed to be crawling here and there, in the sombre light, among the foliated sheets of intense green.

'I cannot convey the sense of abominable desolation that hung over the world. The red eastern sky, the northward blackness, the salt Dead Sea, the stony beach crawling with these foul, slow-stirring monsters, the uniform poisonous-looking green of the lichenous plants, the thin air that hurts one's lungs; all contributed to an appalling effect. I moved on a hundred years, and there was the same red sun – a little larger, a little duller – the same dying sea, the same chill air, and the same crowd of earthy crustacea creeping in and out among the green weed and the red rocks. And in the westward sky I saw a curved pale line like a vast new moon.

'So I travelled, stopping ever and again, in great strides of a thousand years or more, drawn on by the mystery of the earth's fate, watching with a strange fascination the sun grow larger and duller in the westward sky, and the life of the old earth ebb away. At last, more than thirty million years hence, the huge red-hot dome of the sun had come to obscure nearly a tenth part of the darkling heavens. Then I stopped once more, for the crawling multitude of crabs had disappeared, and the red beach, save for its livid green liverworts and lichens, seemed lifeless.

And now it was flecked with white. A bitter cold assailed me. Rare white flakes ever and again came eddying down. To the north-eastward, the glare of snow lay under the starlight of the sable sky, and I could see an undulating crest of hillocks pinkish white. There were fringes of ice along the sea margin, with drifting masses further out; but the main expanse of that salt ocean, all bloody under the eternal sunset, was still unfrozen.

'I looked about me to see if any traces of animal life remained. A certain indefinable apprehension still kept me in the saddle of the machine. But I saw nothing moving, in earth or sky or sea. The green slime on the rocks alone testified that life was not extinct. A shallow sand-bank had appeared in the sea and the water had receded from the beach. I fancied I saw some black object flopping about upon this bank, but it became motionless as I looked at it, and I judged that my eye had been deceived, and that the black object was merely a rock. The stars in the sky were intensely bright and seemed to me to twinkle very little.

'Suddenly I noticed that the circular westward outline of the sun had changed; that a concavity, a bay, had appeared in the curve. I saw this grow larger. For a minute perhaps I stared aghast at this blackness that was creeping over the day, and then I realized that an eclipse was beginning. Either the moon or the planet Mercury was passing across the sun's disk. Naturally, at first I took it to be the moon, but there is much to incline me to believe that what I really saw was the transit of an inner planet passing very near to the earth.

'The darkness grew apace; a cold wind began to blow in freshening gusts from the east, and the showering white flakes in the air increased in number. From the edge of the sea came a ripple and whisper. Beyond these lifeless sounds the world was silent. Silent? It would be hard to convey the stillness of it. All the sounds of man, the bleating of sheep, the cries of birds, the hum of insects, the stir that makes the background of our lives – all that was over. As the darkness thickened, the eddying flakes grew more abundant, dancing before my eyes; and the cold of the air more intense. At last, one by one, swiftly, one after the other, the white peaks of the distant hills vanished into blackness. The breeze rose to a moaning wind. I saw the black central shadow of the eclipse sweeping towards me. In another moment the pale stars alone were visible. All else was rayless obscurity. The sky was absolutely black.

'A horror of this great darkness came on me. The cold, that smote to my marrow, and the pain I felt in breathing, overcame me. I shivered, and a deadly nausea seized me. Then like a red-hot bow in the sky appeared the edge of the sun. I got off the machine to recover myself. I felt giddy and incapable of facing the return journey. As I stood sick and confused I saw again the moving thing upon the shoal – there was no mistake now that it was a moving thing – against the red water of the sea. It was a round thing, the size of a football perhaps, or, it may be, bigger, and tentacles trailed down from it; it seemed black against the weltering blood-red water, and it was hopping fitfully about. Then I felt I was fainting. But a terrible dread of lying helpless in that remote and awful twilight sustained me while I clambered upon the saddle.

'So I came back. For a long time I must have been insensible upon the machine. The blinking succession of the days and nights was resumed, the sun got golden again, the sky blue. I breathed with greater freedom. The fluctuating contours of the land ebbed and flowed. The hands spun backward upon the dials. At last I saw again the dim shadows of houses, the evidences of decadent humanity. These, too, changed and passed, and others came. Presently, when the million dial was at zero, I slackened speed. I began to recognize our own petty and familiar architecture, the thousands hand ran back to the starting-point, the night and day flapped slower and slower. Then the old walls of the laboratory came round me. Very gently, now, I slowed the mechanism down.

'I saw one little thing that seemed odd to me. I think I have told you that when I set out, before my velocity became very high, Mrs. Watchett had walked across the room, travelling, as it seemed to me, like a rocket. As I returned, I passed again across that minute when she traversed the laboratory. But now her every motion appeared to be the exact inversion of her previous ones. The door at the lower end opened, and she glided quietly up the laboratory, back foremost, and disappeared behind the door by which she had previously entered. Just before that I seemed to see Hillyer for a moment; but he passed like a flash.

'Then I stopped the machine, and saw about me again the old familiar laboratory, my tools, my appliances just as I had left them. I got off the thing very shakily, and sat down upon my bench. For several minutes I trembled violently. Then I became calmer. Around me was my old workshop again, exactly as it had been. I might have slept there, and the whole thing have been a dream.

'And yet, not exactly! The thing had started from the south-east corner of the laboratory. It had come to rest again in the north-west, against the wall where you saw it. That gives you the exact distance from my little lawn to the pedestal of the White Sphinx, into which the Morlocks had carried my machine.

'For a time my brain went stagnant. Presently I got up and came through the passage here, limping, because my heel was still painful, and feeling sorely begrimed. I saw the *Pall Mall Gazette* on the table by the door. I found the date was indeed to-day, and looking at the timepiece, saw the hour was almost eight o'clock. I heard your voices and the clatter of plates. I hesitated – I felt so sick and weak. Then I sniffed good wholesome meat, and opened the door on you. You know the rest. I washed, and dined, and now I am telling you the story.

'I know,' he said, after a pause, 'that all this will be absolutely incredible to you. To me the one incredible thing is that I am here to-night in this old familiar room looking into your friendly faces and telling you these strange adventures.'

He looked at the Medical Man. 'No. I cannot expect you to believe it. Take it as a lie – or a prophecy. Say I dreamed it in the workshop. Consider I have been speculating upon the destinies of our race until I have hatched this fiction. Treat my assertion of its truth as a mere stroke of art to enhance its interest. And taking it as a story, what do you think of it?'

He took up his pipe, and began, in his old accustomed manner, to tap with it nervously upon the bars of the grate. There was a momentary stillness. Then chairs began to creak and shoes to scrape upon the carpet. I took my eyes off the Time Traveller's face, and looked round at his audience. They were in the dark, and little spots of colour swam before them. The Medical Man seemed absorbed in the contemplation of our host. The Editor was looking hard at the end of his cigar – the sixth. The Journalist fumbled for his watch. The others, as far as I remember, were motionless.

The Editor stood up with a sigh. 'What a pity it is you're not a writer of stories!' he said, putting his hand on the Time Traveller's shoulder.

'You don't believe it?'

'Well—'

'I thought not.'

The Time Traveller turned to us. 'Where are the matches?' he said. He lit one and spoke over his pipe, puffing. 'To tell you the truth . . . I hardly believe it myself. . . . And yet . . .'

His eye fell with a mute inquiry upon the withered white flowers upon the little table. Then he turned over the hand holding his pipe, and I saw he was looking at some half-healed scars on his knuckles.

The Medical Man rose, came to the lamp, and examined the flowers. 'The gynæceum's odd,' he said. The Psychologist leant forward to see, holding out his hand for a specimen.

'I'm hanged if it isn't a quarter to one,' said the Journalist. 'How shall we get home?'

'Plenty of cabs at the station,' said the Psychologist.

'It's a curious thing,' said the Medical Man; 'but I certainly don't know the natural order of these flowers. May I have them?'

The Time Traveller hesitated. Then suddenly: 'Certainly not.'

'Where did you really get them?' said the Medical Man.

The Time Traveller put his hand to his head. He spoke like one who was trying to keep hold of an idea that eluded him. 'They were put into my pocket by Weena, when I travelled into Time.' He stared round the room. 'I'm damned if it isn't all going. This room and you and the atmosphere of every day is too much for my memory. Did I ever make a Time Machine, or a model of a Time Machine? Or is it all only a dream? They say life is a dream, a precious poor dream at times – but I can't stand another that won't fit. It's madness. And where did the dream come from? . . . I must look at that machine. If there *is* one!'

He caught up the lamp swiftly, and carried it, flaring red, through the door into the corridor. We followed him. There in the flickering light of the lamp was the machine sure enough, squat, ugly, and askew; a thing of brass, ebony, ivory, and translucent glimmering quartz. Solid to the touch – for I put out my hand and felt the rail of it – and with brown spots and smears upon the ivory, and bits of grass and moss upon the lower parts, and one rail bent awry.

The Time Traveller put the lamp down on the bench, and ran his hand along the damaged rail. 'It's all right now,' he said. 'The story I told you was true. I'm sorry to have brought you out here in the cold.' He took up the lamp, and, in an absolute silence, we returned to the smoking-room.

He came into the hall with us and helped the Editor on with his coat. The Medical Man looked into his face and, with a certain hesitation, told him he was suffering from overwork, at which he laughed hugely. I remember him standing in the open doorway, bawling good night.

I shared a cab with the Editor. He thought the tale a 'gaudy lie'. For my own part I was unable to come to a conclusion. The story was so fantastic and incredible, the telling so credible and sober. I lay awake most of the night thinking about it. I determined to go next day and see the Time Traveller again. I was told he was in the laboratory, and being on easy terms in the house, I went up to him. The laboratory, however, was empty. I stared for a minute at the Time Machine and put out my hand and touched the lever. At that the squat substantial-looking mass swayed like a bough shaken by the wind. Its instability startled me extremely, and I had a queer reminiscence of the childish days when I used to be forbidden to meddle. I came back through the corridor. The Time Traveller met me in the smoking-room. He was coming from the house. He had a small camera under one arm and a knapsack under the other. He laughed when he saw me, and gave me an elbow to shake. 'I'm frightfully busy,' said he, 'with that thing in there.'

'But is it not some hoax?' I said. 'Do you really travel through time?'

'Really and truly I do.' And he looked frankly into my eyes. He hesitated. His eye wandered about the room. 'I only want half an hour,' he said. 'I know why you came, and it's awfully good of you. There's some magazines here. If you'll stop to lunch I'll prove you this time travelling up to the hilt, specimens and all. If you'll forgive my leaving you now?'

I consented, hardly comprehending then the full import of his words, and he nodded and went on down the corridor. I heard the door of the laboratory slam, seated myself in a chair, and took up a daily paper. What was he going to do before lunch-time? Then suddenly I was reminded by an advertisement that I had promised to meet Richardson, the publisher, at two. I looked at my watch, and saw that I could barely save that engagement. I got up and went down the passage to tell the Time Traveller.

As I took hold of the handle of the door I heard an exclamation, oddly truncated at the end, and a click and a thud. A gust of air whirled round me as I opened the door, and from within came the sound of broken glass falling on the floor. The

Time Traveller was not there. I seemed to see a ghostly, indistinct figure sitting in a whirling mass of black and brass for a moment — a figure so transparent that the bench behind with its sheets of drawings was absolutely distinct; but this phantasm vanished as I rubbed my eyes. The Time Machine had gone. Save for a subsiding stir of dust, the further end of the laboratory was empty. A pane of the skylight had, apparently, just been blown in.

I felt an unreasonable amazement. I knew that something strange had happened, and for the moment could not distinguish what the strange thing might be. As I stood staring, the door into the garden opened, and the man-servant appeared.

We looked at each other. Then ideas began to come. 'Has Mr. — gone out that way?' said I.

'No, sir. No one has come out this way. I was expecting to find him here.'

At that I understood. At the risk of disappointing Richardson I stayed on, waiting for the Time Traveller; waiting for the second, perhaps still stranger story, and the specimens and photographs he would bring with him. But I am beginning now to fear that I must wait a lifetime. The Time Traveller vanished three years ago. And, as everybody knows now, he has never returned.

EPILOGUE

One cannot choose but wonder. Will he ever return? It may be that he swept back into the past, and fell among the blood-drinking, hairy savages of the Age of Unpolished Stone; into the abysses of the Cretaceous Sea; or among the grotesque saurians, the huge reptilian brutes of the Jurassic times. He may even now – if I may use the phrase – be wandering on some plesiosaurus-haunted Oolitic coral reef, or beside the lonely saline lakes of the Triassic Age. Or did he go forward, into one of the nearer ages, in which men are still men, but with the riddles of our own time answered and its wearisome problems solved? Into the manhood of the race: for I, for my own part, cannot think that these latter days of weak experiment, fragmentary theory, and mutual discord are indeed man's culminating time! I say, for my own part. He, I know – for the question had been discussed among us long before the Time Machine was made – thought but cheerlessly of the Advancement of Mankind, and saw in the growing pile of civilisation only a foolish heaping that must inevitably fall back upon and destroy its makers in the end. If that is so, it remains for us to live as though it were not so. But to me the future is still black and blank – is a vast ignorance, lit at a few casual places by the memory of his story. And I have by me, for my comfort, two strange white flowers – shrivelled now, and brown and flat and brittle – to witness that even when mind and strength had gone, gratitude and a mutual tenderness still lived on in the heart of man.

APPENDIX

In his Preface to the Atlantic edition of *The Time Machine* Wells writes that W. E. Henley wanted 'to put a little "writing" into the tale',* but that he eventually prevailed over Henley and cut out the additions. I do not interpret this as meaning that Henley added his own words to the *New Review* version, but that he influenced Wells in the course of what he thought should be written. What follows was included in the text of the *New Review* version, but cut from the Heinemann edition of 1895. It was originally in Chapter Eleven p. 72, after 'into futurity', at the end of paragraph 1.

Very cautiously, for I remembered my former headlong fall, I began to reverse my motion. Slower and slower went the circling hands until the thousands one seemed motionless and the daily one was no longer a mere mist upon its scale. Still slower, until the grey haze around me became distincter and dim outlines of an undulating waste grew visible.

I stopped. I was on a bleak moorland, covered with a sparse vegetation, and grey with a thin hoarfrost. The time was midday, the orange sun, shorn of its effulgence, brooded near the meridian in a sky of drabby grey. Only a few black bushes broke the monotony of the scene. The great buildings of the decadent men among whom, it seemed to me, I had been so recently, had vanished and left no trace: not a mound even marked their position. Hill and valley, sea and river all, under the wear and work of the rain and frost, had melted into new forms. No doubt, too, the rain and snow had long since washed out the Morlock tunnels. A nipping breeze stung my hands and face. So far as I could see there were neither hills, nor trees, nor rivers: only an uneven stretch of cheerless plateau.

Then suddenly a dark bulk rose out of the moor, something that gleamed like a serrrated row of iron plates, and vanished

* H.G.W, *Atlantic Edition* of the *Collected Works*, 1924, vol. 1. pp. xxi–xxii.

almost immediately in a depression. And then I became aware of a number of faint-grey things, coloured to almost the exact tint of the frost-bitten soil, which were browsing here and there upon its scanty grass, and running to and fro. I saw one jump with a sudden start, and then my eye detected perhaps a score of them. At first I thought they were rabbits, or some small breed of kangaroo. Then, as one came hopping near me, I perceived that it belonged to neither of these groups. It was plantigrade, its hind legs rather the longer: it was tailless, and covered with a straight greyish hair that thickened about the head into a Skye terrier's mane. As I had understood that in the Golden Age man had killed out almost all the other animals, sparing only a few of the more ornamental, I was naturally curious about the creatures. They did not seem afraid of me, but browsed on, much as rabbits would do in a place unfrequented by men; and it occurred to me that I might perhaps secure a specimen.

I got off the machine, and picked up a big stone. I had scarcely done so when one of the little creatures came within easy range. I was so lucky as to hit it on the head, and it rolled over at once and lay motionless. I ran to it at once. It remained still, almost as if it were killed. I was surprised to see that the thing had five feeble digits to both its fore and hind feet – the fore feet, indeed, were almost as human as the fore feet of a frog. It had, moreover, a roundish head, with a projecting forehead and forward-looking eyes, obscured by its lank hair. A disagreeable apprehension flashed across my mind. As I knelt down and seized my capture intending to examine its teeth and other anatomical points which might show human characteristics, the metallic-looking object, to which I have already alluded, reappeared above a ridge in the moor, coming towards me and making a strange clattering sound as it came. Forthwith the grey animals about me began to answer with a short, weak yelping – as if of terror – and bolted off in a direction opposite to that from which this new creature approached. They must have hidden in burrows or behind bushes and tussocks, for in a moment not one of them was visible.

I rose to my feet, and stared at this grotesque monster. I can only describe it by comparing it to a centipede. It stood about three feet high and had a long segmented body, perhaps thirty feet long, with curiously overlapping greenish-black plates. It seemed to crawl upon a multitude of feet, looping its body as it advanced. Its blunt round head, with a polygonal arrangement of black eye spots, carried two flexible, writhing, horn-like antennae. It was coming along, I should judge, at a pace of about eight or ten miles an hour, and it left me little time for thinking. Leaving my grey animal, or grey man, whichever it was, on the ground. I set off for the machine. Halfway I paused, regretting that abandonment, but a glance over my shoulder destroyed any such regret. When I gained the machine the monster was scarce fifty yards away. It was certainly not a vertebrated animal. It had no snout, and its mouth was fringed with jointed dark-coloured plates. But I did not care for a nearer view.

I traversed one day and stopped again, hoping to find the colossus gone and some vestige of my victim; but, I should judge, the giant centipede did not trouble itself about bones. At any rate both had vanished. The faintly human touch of these little creatures perplexed me greatly. If you come to think, there is no reason why a degenerate humanity should not come at last to differentiate into as many species as the descendants of the mud fish who fathered all the land vertebrates. I saw no more of any insect colossus, as to my thinking the segmented creature must have been. Evidently the physiological difficulty that at present keeps all the insects small had been surmounted at last, and this division of the animal kingdom had arrived at the long-awaited supremacy which its enormous energy and vitality deserve. I made several attempts to kill or capture another of the greyish vermin, but none of my missiles were so successful as my first; and, after perhaps a dozen disappointing throws, that left my arm aching, I felt a gust of irritation at my folly in coming so far into futurity without weapons or equipment. I resolved to run on for one glimpse of the still remoter future – one peep into the deeper abysm of time – and then to return to you and my own epoch. Once more I remounted the machine, and once more the world grew hazy and grey.

WELLS AND HIS CRITICS

The Time Machine was Wells's first novel. He had been in print, as a professional writer, since 1891 when the *Fortnightly Review* published his article 'The Rediscovery of the Unique'. His first book had been *A Text Book of Biology* in 1893, which was to remain in print for over forty years. He was, by this time, living by his writing.

The Review of Reviews, in an issue published two months before the book edition of *The Time Machine*, but clearly responding to the serialization then running, termed Wells: '. . . a man of genius [whose imagination is] as gruesome as that of Poe'.[1]

The Daily Chronicle found no fault with the book:

> . . . since the appearance of [*Dr Jekyll and Mr Hyde*] we have had nothing in the domain of fantasy so bizarre as this 'invention' by Mr H. G. Wells. For his central idea Mr Wells may be indebted to some previously published narrative suggestion, but if so we must confess ourselves entirely unacquainted with it. And so far as our knowledge goes he has produced in fiction that rarity which Solomon declared to be not merely rare but non-existent – a 'new thing under the sun'.[2]

The 'backlash' – if it can fairly be called that – was already under way, however. In *The Spectator* an anonymous reviewer rightly saw Wells as delivering a warning to contemporary society. The reviewer takes a strongly moral line, objecting at every stage to Wells's projected human evolution, to a resoundingly Christian conclusion:

> But it is not in some 'unknown Power's employ' that we move along this 'rigorous line'. On the contrary, it is in the employ of a power which has revealed itself in the Incarnation and the Cross. And we may expect with the utmost confidence that if the earth is

still in existence in the year 802,701 AD, either the AD will mean a great deal more than it means now, or else its inhabitants will be neither Eloi nor Morlocks. For in that case evil passions will by that time have led to the extinction of races spurred and pricked on by conscience and yet so frivolous or malignant. Yet Mr Wells's fanciful and lively dream is well worth reading, if only because it will draw attention to the great moral and religious factors in human nature which he appears to ignore.[3]

Fellow novelist Israel Zangwill took the problems and paradoxes of time travel very seriously, speaking of the 'absurdity of any attempt to grapple with time' – and it is arguable that by 'creating' a time machine, and clothing his work in the garb of science (earlier writers depicting time travel favoured dreams, comas, blows to the head or plain magic) Wells invoked the precision and erudition of Zangwill. He is, however, ultimately dismissive, ultimately misled by the 'fact' of time travel, from its purpose:

> ... despite some ingenious metaphysics, worthy of the inventor of the Eleatic paradoxes, Mr Wells's Time Machine, which traverses time (viewed as the Fourth Dimension of Space) backwards or forwards, remains an amusing fantasy.[4]

Within three years Wells had produced so much that it was possible for a writer of thirty-two to have 'retrospectives' written about his work. The following was written by his old NSS friend, Richard Gregory, whom Wells frequently consulted over matters of accuracy in his science fiction:

> Many writers of fiction have gathered material from the fairy-land of science, and have used it in the construction of literary fabrics, but none have done it more successfully than Mr H. G. Wells. It is often easy to understand the cause of failure. The material may be used in such a way that there seems to be no connection between it and the background upon which it is seen: it may be so prominent that the threads with which it ought to harmonize are thrown into obscurity; or (and this is the worst of all) it may be employed by a writer whose knowledge of natural phenomena is not sufficient to justify his working with scientific colour. Mr Wells makes none of these mistakes. Upon a groundwork of scientific fact, his vivid imagination and exceptional powers enable

him to erect a structure which readers can find pleasure in contemplating.

The Time Machine – considered by the majority of scientific readers to be Mr Wells's best work – showed at once that a writer has arisen who was not only familiar with scientific facts, but also knew them intimately enough to present a view of the future.[5]

Long before he was fifty Wells was world-famous. Yet the novels of his middle age were not well received. Set this alongside the fact that his science fiction has always run the risk of relegation to children's reading, and it becomes difficult to find English critics of the time writing positively or constructively about his work, however much they appreciate Wells the 'statesman'. Indeed, it could be argued that the sheer fame of Wells, his position as the author of best-selling non-fiction such as *The Outline of History*, got between the man and the fiction, the fiction and the critic. One of the best appraisals of Wells came from abroad, from the Russian writer Yevgeni Zamyatin:

The motifs of the Wellsian urban fairy tales are essentially the same as those encountered in all other fairy tales: the invisible cap, the flying carpet, the bursting grass, the self-setting table-cloth, dragons, giants, gnomes, mermaids, and man-eating monsters. But the difference between his tales and, let us say, ours, is the difference between the psychology of a Poshkenonian and that of a Londoner: our Russian Poshkenonian sits down at the window and waits until the invisible cap and the flying carpet come to him magically ... the Londoner ... relies on himself. He sits down at the drawing-board, takes the slide rule and calculates a flying carpet. He goes to the laboratory, fires the electric furnace and invents the bursting grass. The Poshkenonian reconciles himself to his wonders happening in twenty-seven lands and forty kingdoms away. The Londoner wants his wonders today, right now, right here. And therefore chooses the trustiest road to his fairy tales – a road paved with astronomic, physical, and chemical formulas, a road rolled flat and solid by the cast-iron laws of the exact sciences. This may seem paradoxical at first – exact science and fairy tale, precision and fantasy. But it is so, and must be so. For a myth is always, openly or implicitly, connected with religion, and the religion of the modern city is precise science. Hence, the natural link between the newest urban myth, urban fairy tale, and science. And I do not know whether there is a single major branch of the exact sciences that has not been reflected in Wells's fantastic novels. Mathematics, astronomy, astrophysics, physics, chemistry, medicine, physiology, bacteriology, mechanics, electrotechnology, aviation. Almost all of Wells's fairy tales are built upon brilliant and unexpected scientific paradoxes. All his myths are as logical as mathematical equations. And this is why we, modern men, we, skeptics, are conquered by these logical fantasies, this is why they command out attention and win our belief.[6]

I would argue Wells had to wait another forty years for criticism as acute as that in English.

A quarter of a century later, there is a valuable perspective to be found in the work of the French writer Antonina Vallentin. She takes a sideways look at the Englishness of Wells, as only an outsider could, and it is a disturbing version – one I doubt would be expressed by any English writer on Wells as early as 1950. So much English writing on Wells at that time was on Wells the man, simply remembering him. This is different.

The 'Time Traveller' was set firmly in realistic surroundings, and linked to everyday life by innumerable ties, such as were familiar to all readers. Wells had realized that the more fantastic the story he told, the more commonplace must be its setting. His ability to create such a commonplace setting was quite new, a year ago, or even less, he could not have done it, but now he did it with masterly ease. *The Time Machine* glitters with the same surface irony as 'The Stolen Bacillus'. But below the surface are depths of gloom and cruel despair. What can have been the matter with the eyes of his contemporaries, that they could overlook the chief problem raised by the book? The notion of a fourth dimension must have dazzled them so completely that they never went on to investigate the nature of the theories that Wells set forth with such relish. His fireworks hid the murky background from their eyes. The book had a curiously sadistic strain, so evident that one wonders whether it can really have escaped even the English, who look upon *Alice in Wonderland*, with its strong under-current of cruelty, as an ideal book for children.

The death of little Wena, [sic] the greatly loving childwife, in the night, uplifted on the crimson canopy of flame that drifts away into shreds leaving a plume of smoke rising toward the tiny, far-distant stars, while the darkness swarms with white, flabby forms that crawl toward the still, doll-like figure, is an episode so soaked in horror as to be almost physically sickening.

When the book first came out, it reminded some people of Edgar Allan Poe. But Poe's horrific atmosphere, and the shudder which he delighted to provoke in his readers, were for him not only a means but an end, whereas Wells directed his horrors toward a definite aim. The purely imaginative form serves to camouflage what his time called a story with a purpose.[7]

When Wells died, just short of his eightieth birthday in 1946, *The Times* caught the power of his impact in a single sentence:

> There was a time when Wells spoke more clearly than any other man to the youth of the world.

Many writers who read Wells's science fiction in childhood, when it was new or almost-new, have recalled the impact he made upon them. V. S. Pritchett (born 1900):

> I have lately read all those scientific books from *The Time Machine* to *The War in the Air* and it has been a refreshing experience. There was a time, one realises, when science was fun. For the food of the gods is more entertaining that the prosaic efficacy of vitamins; the tripods of the Martians are more engaging than tanks. And then, here you have Wells at his best, eagerly displaying the inventive imagination, first with the news and at play, with an artist's innocence. Here you see his intoxicated response – a response that was lacking in his contemporaries – to the front-page situation of his time, and here you meet his mastery of the art of story-telling, the bounce and resource of it. Above all, in these early books, you catch Wells in the act, his very characteristic act, of breaking down mean barriers and setting you free. He has burst out himself and he wants everyone else to do the same. 'Why', cries the engineer in *The Food of the Gods* – the poorest of these books – 'Why don't we do what we want to do?'

> For that matter, I have never read any book by H. G. Wells, early or late, which did not start off by giving me an exhilarating sense of personal freedom. Every inhibition I ever had faded from me as I read. Of course, after such a high, hard bounce one comes down again. The answer to the engineer's question is that we do not do what we want to do because we want to do opposite things

at the same time. Yet that infectious Wellsian sense of freedom was not all anarchy, romantic ebullience or Utopian uplift. That freedom was a new fact in our environment; one pays for everything – that is all.[8]

And J. B. Priestley (born 1894):

I have read – or tried to read – a great deal of contemporary Science Fiction ... I hope I do not appear prejudiced in favour of a man for whom I had I had an affection just 'this side of idolatry', if I say that not one of these contemporary writers combines all the qualities found in the early Wells. They never seem to me to achieve his unique mixture of an imaginative scientific vision and the storyteller's art. Even when it succeeds as brilliant satire, their work is not as deeply rooted in human experience as Wells' best tales are. They are not in fact expressing themselves from a level of personality as deep as his. Though he himself would have denied this hotly, there is really more of the essential H. G. Wells in his early Science Fiction than there is in his later sociological novels and innumerable treatises on the education and organization of mankind.

Like almost all great writers, Wells was a sharply divided man, especially during the first half of his life. The opposites were at war in his rich personality, and out of this deep hidden conflict came his energy and imaginative force. His training and his conscious outlook were scientific, rational, intellectual, and fiercely contemptuous of disorder and muddle and what seemed to him outworn traditional values. The other and less conscious half of him belonged, almost in spite of himself, to imaginative literature and a quite different set of values. To the end of his life – and I say this out of personal experience, for during the later 1930s and the earlier 1940s we were friends – there was in the depths of his personality this conflict between two different sets of values, between the aggressive and impatient scientific rationalist and the imaginative, humorous, tolerant man of literary genius. As the world scene darkened, and one appalling war merely brought an uneasy peace that inevitably produced a second war, the educationalist in him, the propagandist for a scientifically based international order, defeated the imaginative creator in him; but his earlier work represents a kind of balance between these two – not a conscious agreement between them but a collaboration largely unconscious – and it is to this, I maintain, that his early tales owe their fascination and force.[9]

Among Wells's obituaries was this from another who shared the feelings of Pritchett and Priestley, George Orwell:

Wells belonged to the generation which had won the battle for freedom of thought against Victorian obscurantism, and by temperament he was an optimist. Up to 1914 he probably believed – though with fairly frequent misgivings – that mankind was assured of a reasonable and orderly future. The war of 1914–18 shook his confidence and from then on he became increasingly intent on preaching the need for world organization ... No other writer of our time, at any rate no English writer, has so deeply influenced his contemporaries as Wells. He was so big a figure, he played so large a part in forming our picture of the world, that in agreeing or disagreeing with his ideas we are apt to forget his purely literary achievement. In his own eyes it was a secondary, almost an unimportant thing. He had faults of intellect and of character, but very few writers have ever had less literary vanity.[10]

The nineteen-fifties were lean years for the appreciation of Wells. The huge Pelican *Guide to English Literature* all but ignores him. Those that knew him had already set down their recollections – Chesterton, Rebecca West, Shaw, among others, all had something to say about Wells. And, looking at Conrad and Lawrence, the first ten years after a writer's death tend to see them neglected. However, the fifties did see a 'detached' life of Wells, a very lively biography by Vincent Brome:

From his inexhaustible treasure house of ideas he worked at now one, now another novel, with none of the finesse of Henry James – 'Oh what an artist spoilt,' James said of him – but shapelessly, with a huge exciting energy which slapped scenes down on paper and didn't gravely mind if there were ragged ends or characters lost in the scramble, so long as they were alive and conveyed his essential ideas. In the beginning it was ideas that mattered more than characters. *The Time Machine* (1894) lived by the grace of scientific gods, *the Stolen Bacillus* and *The Island of Dr. Moreau* (1896), *The Star* and *The Invisible Man* (1897) all dabbled in the scientific occult, taking the laws of science far beyond their bounds, yet never so much as to fuss broad-minded scientists, and

never so little as to make dull reading. Wells knew just how to
unlock the excitements, the imaginative worlds, buried beneath
dull scientific data. He also knew the necessity of creating commonplace everyday people and incidents very much of this earth,
alongside the great streaming fantasy world in which he placed
them. 'For the writer of fantastic stories to help the reader play
the game properly,' he wrote, 'he must help him, in every possible
unobtrusive way, to *domesticate* the impossible hypothesis ...'
The plausible illusion must be swiftly established with an air of
ordinariness, and before incredulity overtook the reader he must
be swept along by the story until he had surrendered completely
to the element of magic. It was the modern mode of an old
technique. A talk with the alchemist, the devil, the magician had
yielded fantastic stories before. The Frankenstein monster had
come out of some such primitive furnace. Wells substituted the
current scientific patter of the day, skilfully turned theories of time
and interstellar space to similar account. 'I simply brought the
fetish stuff up to date and made it as near actual theory as possible
...' But he also, with boundless vitality and immense humanity,
created characters who saw life from their new angle with all the
emotional authenticity of 'one of us', and sometimes with an
emotional magic which left a glow in the reader's mind. It did not
always happen ... [but] ... sometimes he tilted up the cart of his
mind and out rumbled stone, rubbish, and good rich beautiful soil
to mount under the astonished reader's eye, into yet another
chapter, if not book.'[11]

Wells began again to be taken seriously with the work of
Bernard Bergonzi, whose study of the early science fiction
appeared in 1961:

The opposition of Eloi and Morlocks can be interpreted in terms
of the late nineteenth-century class struggle, but it also reflects an
opposition between aestheticism and utilitarianism, pastoralism
and technology, contemplation and action, and ultimately, and
least specifically, between beauty and ugliness, and light and
darkness. The book not only embodies the tensions and dilemmas
of its time, but others peculiar to Wells himself, which a few years
later were to make him cease to be an artist and become a
propagandist. Since the tensions are imaginatively but not intellec-
tually resolved we find that a note of irony becomes increasingly

pronounced as the Traveller persists in his disconcerting exploration of the world in which he has found himself. *The Time
Machine* is not only a myth, but an ironic myth, like many other
considerable works of modern literature. And despite the com-
plexity of its thematic elements, Wells's art is such that the story
is a skilfully wrought imaginative whole, a single image.[12]

In the 1970s Norman and Jeanne Mackenzie produced a fuller
life of Wells, and in the extract that follows pinpoint the mood
that created *The Time Machine*:

The sense of an impending apocalypse pervades all the scientific
romances. Wells shared this sense with many of his contemporaries, but it was accentuated in his work by the important and
equally gloomy influences on the way he perceived the world and
his own place in it.
    The first was the brooding sense of impending collapse, both of
the business and the family which hung over Atlas House. This
was intensified by his persistent ill-health and his fears of an early
death. It was but a short step from his fears of his own extinction
to a more generalised fear of the Extinction of Man. The second
was the effect of his childhood religion, which made Wells
peculiarly susceptible to any theory of biology or cosmogony
which suggested that man's place in nature might be precarious,
and that a way of avoiding the last of all judgements might lie –
in Huxley's phrase – in his success in 'checking the cosmic process
at every step'. And, thirdly, at South Kensington, Wells not only
absorbed Huxley's pessimistic gloss on evolutionary theory, but
he was also affected by the work of Kelvin and others who insisted
that the law of entropy would eventually lead to a cooling of the
sun and the reduction of the planets to a system of dead matter
whirling in the nothingness of space.[13]

In 1983 Wells's youngest son Anthony West wrote a biography
of his father. It contains the most vivid account of the impact of
Uppark's subterranean world on Wells:

The room was buried deeply in the ground ... The whole
basement floor shared its qualities, as did the huge underground
kitchen buried beneath a shrubbery at some distance from the
main building, and connected with it by a tunnel – a long passage

dimly lit in the daytime by light from overhead skylights made secure by prison-like metal gratings.

My father's initial response to his discovery of this nether world of underprivilege below Uppark had been one of blind rage. This was because it had been my grandmother's most persistent complaint against my grandfather that his lack of consideration for her condemned her to spend the greater part of her day every day below ground level in the basement kitchen of Atlas House, a room that borrowed its light from a pit covered by a metal grating set into the pavement of Bromley's High Street. It had infuriated my father to find that his mother had tried to destroy all his hopes, and to condemn him to be something less than a lackey, on the pretext that she was seizing her last chance to escape from her underground servitude, when it had been her intention, all along, to install herself in this larger version of the same thing. His bottled-up feelings on this score, mingled with others, even more powerful, concerning the fundamentals of the relationship between his parents, had finally burst out into the open in his descriptions of the loathly caverns inhabited by the light-fearing Morlocks in *The Time Machine*.[14]

Michael Moorcock – the prolific modern writer of science fiction – writing in 1993, placed Wells in the context of the reading and writing of the nineties:

Time-travel stories, like all kinds of speculative romance, were popular with late Victorian readers. Edwin Lester Arnold's *Phra the Phoenician* had proceeded through Time by a process of reincarnation and Mark Twain's Yankee had gone back to the Court of King Arthur via a blow on the head. Like F. Anstey's *Tormalin's Time Cheques* (1891), such stories were often used to examine human society and find it wanting. Most travellers had merely to fall asleep, a Rip Van Winkle, to wake up a century or millennia hence, while Bellamy's *Looking Backward* had employed the original notion of placing the narrator in the future and reviewing our coming history as his past. In spite of all this and his own modest claims, Wells's *Time Machine* stands out immediately as something different. As it appeared, month by month, through the first half of 1895, it became a talking point. W. T. Stead's influential *Review of Reviews* called Wells 'a man of genius'. James, Meredith, Conrad and Hardy all recognized a peer. Publishers and editors began to court him and humorists began to satirize him. He could write to his parents that he had 'arrived'.

While improving Wells's fortunes radically, *The Time Machine* was to have an effect on the popular imagination not unlike the film *2001: A Space Odyssey* some seventy years later. It established a public vision of the future, a powerful myth in which human beings evolve into something alien. As he would from now until his film *Things to Come* in 1935, he issued a clear warning: go on as we are now and we are doomed to devolve to the level of brutes and from brutes back to the mud from which we came. In scenes left out of the book version he emphasized this point, describing the process of devolution following the time of the Morlocks. If his motives were Dante's, to show us Hell so that we might avoid it, and his methods were consciously borrowed from Swift, the author's natural optimism is implicit in his decision to write the story. There is no misanthropy in Wells, only distress. It is his characters who despair of dissuading us from our cruel follies.

That issue of the *New Review* for January 1895 is full of excellent journalism. Henley was an impeccable editor, offering his readers only the best. And yet one is immediately struck by the economy, the modernity of Wells's writing and it is not at all surprising that so many recognized his unique gifts. Admirers have pointed out the skill with which he allows us to use our own imagination, describing the Time Traveller's laboratory in precise detail but giving only the vaguest description of the machine; conjuring up other people's visions of the future in order to dismiss those detailed pictures as unlikely – and certainly nothing *he* has observed; offering powerful images of the planet in its decadent and dying years, evoking all the Gothic *frisson* of ruins and loss. He combines the unique personal vision of a Bunyan or a Blake with vivid, economical prose and a driving urgency to alert the world to its moral and physical danger. His language is given further authority by its use of scientific terms. His methods are novel but his instincts have much in common with Jeremiah. He is an authentic original and *The Time Machine* continues to define and influence all those stories that came after it, which have never equalled it.[15]

There are a limited number of models for future-paradise: Medieval (of which Arthurian is a variation), much favoured by the Pre-Raphaelites; Greek, which Wells uses in *The Time Machine* – indeed it is one of the clues to the nature of Eloi society that causes the Traveller to so misread them; and Biblical, which is anybody's guess and is usually clothed in one of the former. Most paradises are rural, to accord with the original – but on occasion they are urban and Wells, for one, created an urban paradise. Malcolm Muggeridge, writing in 1939, responded to Wells's most successful late venture, the eventual mega-city paradise, the triumphant optimism – almost the last such in his life – of the film *Things to Come*, scripted by Wells himself *from* (in the loosest sense) his novel, and produced by the greatest *English* (again, in the loosest sense) film-maker of the thirties, Alexander Korda. Whilst Muggeridge sticks to the film as his issue, the piece implicitly criticizes the science-fiction 'tradition' of creating future-worlds, and hence a large part of Wells's literary output:

> *The Shape of Things to Come* ... holds out the prospect of a world full of charm, correctly shaded lipstick and interchangeable employers and employees. Golden youths and maidens in white silken shorts and open-necked shirts live delectable, amorous lives, provided by science with innumerable conveniences and play-things, shooting through the air at immense speed, falling without self-consciousness into each others hygienic arms, with no jealous squall or inward groan to disturb their bliss ... In Mr Wells too the contemporary mood is made manifest. He has succeeded in giving the harsh materialism in which his own life is rooted, a glow of righteousness and joy. Prosperity, once regarded as an end in itself, he has endowed with transcendental qualities, adding unto it benevolence and eroticism. Bank balances dissolve into embraces, factory chimneys blossom like flowers, and company directors discard their black coats and put on white silk, take off their top-hats to twine bay leaves in their hair. The black coated worker becomes white coated.[16]

Muggeridge goes on to dub Wells 'the prophet of romantic materialism' and to damn him with propagation of the falsehood that the failure of increased wealth to produce increased happiness is a correctable fault rather than 'a fundamental fallacy'. But it is more sinister. It supplants, for Muggeridge, the King-dom of Heaven, by offering a fatuously easy version here on earth. But there are teeth to his critique of future-worlds; in the next chapter he remarks upon a documentary made by Wells's collaborator Julian Huxley, depicting the evolution of man. The futureman and futurewoman are nymph-like, blonde, balletic and rendered barely modest by discretely placed gauze. I have not seen the film, but if Muggeridge was right it epitomizes the cliché of the Utopian future – the common bowdlerization of Wells, the over-optimization of his largely pessimistic vision – these are the Eloi as Hollywood saw them, the Thals of Dr Who and countless other sci-fi visions. It prompts me to ask . . . when did the future become blonde? Why does it always wear sandals? Why does it have such an aversion to trousers? And, as Peter Cook once put it, when did bits of gauze stop floating so conveniently in the air?

In 1928 Herbert Read used Wells as an example in the chapter on Fantasy in his *English Prose Style*:

> A 'Utopia', or description of a fantastical country and its civilization, might well exhibit all the characteristics of pure Fantasy, but rarely does so because the writer has some ulterior or satirical moral aim, which aim directs his composition, fixes it in space and time, gives it a basis of subjective intolerance. Such objections apply to *Utopia* itself, to *News from Nowhere* and *The Dream of John Ball*, to *Erewhon* and *A Crystal Age*. They do not apply to the fantasies of H. G. Wells, who comes as near as any modern writer to a sense of pure Fantasy. He errs, as in *The Time Machine*, by imparting to his fantasies a pseudo-scientific logicality; it is as though, having conceived one arbitrary fantasy he were compelled by the habits of his scientific training to work out the consequences of his fantasy. Real fantasy is bolder than this; it dispenses with all logic and habit and relies on the force of wonder alone.[17]

This is startling to consider. Rarely has a perceptive critic – which Read was – read Wells so clearly, whilst so utterly missing the point. It contrasts with the work of Raymond Williams, in his Cambridge lectures in the 1960s. Half a century on Williams is better placed to see that in Wells which was so different from what had gone before, to see the sum of the parts that were fantasy, sociological realism and 'pseudo-scientific logicality'. While Read seeks continuity of form, Williams sees 1895 as a watershed for the novel; his perception of the elements in Wells, whilst expressed very differently, is not unlike Read's, but his conclusion is wholly different:

> 1895 ... in the late 1870s, the early 1880s, the Victorian period ended ... Socially, culturally, economically, politically, a new phase of our history began. It is quite identifiable, from the late 1870s to the war in 1914. And what is there as scattered accumulating evidence, over two decades, reaches a critical point in the 1890s. The last year of Hardy, the year of *Jude the Obscure*, is also the first year of Wells, the year of *The Time Machine* ... something important and decisive was happening in that period to what can be called the English tradition ... For the predominant formula at the time he was writing was not only a traditional community – the country-house world of Bladesover [in *Tono Bungay*]. It was also the inherited, the shaping form of the novel.

Now it is here, really, that the split takes place. To accept that world, that form, was in a very deep way to accept its consciousness. Of course with every kind of qualification and refinement; an intense pressure, a self-conscious and intricate pressure within that imaginary, imaginative circle. To question the circle itself, to examine the relations which composed it – profound relations of property, income, work, education – was not only radical in overt ways – asking radical questions, giving radical opinions. It was a break in texture where consciousness itself was determined; an assault, or so it seemed, not only on the form of the novel but on an idea, *the* idea, of literature itself.

And this is Wells's importance ... He failed in the end; he emigrated to World Government as clearly as Lawrence to Mexico. But until 1914, until that real break that went beyond him, not only a restless energy – fashion is prepared to concede that to outsiders – but a creative energy, and a creative energy in fiction. His simplest successes are of course what are called the romances (that's placing again, very like 'provincial'). He avoids tearing that seamless cloth, that traditional texture of the novel, by taking his consciousness of change – his sense of history and of the urgency of transformation – outside that social fiction, that intensive realism, where in existing circumstances such questions could never be put; or rather, could be put as questions but could never become actions. The Morlocks and the Eloi at the end of *The Time Machine*; the alteration of consciousness in the passing of the Comet; the disturbance of conventions by the invisible man:

these were real ways through, in an otherwise reconciling world. Kipps and Mr Polly, men on the run from the system: there we see the alternative: and irrepressible humour and energy, but not the humour and energy of Dickens, transforming a world; only the endlessly self-conscious, self-consciously perky, the almost apologetic assertion – over the shoulder, behind the hand of a right to live.[18]

The following is the most succinct account I have read of Wells the writer:

I once told H. G. Wells and, after reflection, he agreed with my analysis, that at least two people struggled inside him, Herbert and George. Bert reacted; George dreamed. Bert was often cross, but, because he was a man of genius, he worked off his irritation in splendid stories about the frustrations of innumerable other Herberts who were bullied and patronised as he had been . . .

. . . When George took over from Bert, books like Kipps and Mr Polly were born. Here experience has passed through the magic process, the alchemy which turns revolt into art. George Ponderevo is Pip in Great Expectations, despised but striving for Estella, or David Copperfield barking his shins against the rungs of the social ladder. Kipps and Mr Polly are in origin stories, not only about Wells himself, when he was for two unhappy periods a draper's assistant, 'living in', as the system of shop slavery used to be called, yearning for a dream life of adventure, for the companionship of gorgeous women, seen in daily life only too well protected by immaculate males in unattainable evening dress, but they had been transformed into universalised figures, Dickensian in their individuality and permanence. And Bert was sure to turn up again. He couldn't stand criticism. He could be unbelievably touchy and tetchy.[19]

References

1. Unsigned article, *Review of Reviews*, March 1895.
2. Unsigned review, *Daily Chronicle*, 27 July 1895.
3. Richard Holt Hutton, unsigned review, *The Spectator*, 13 July 1895.
4. Israel Zangwill, *Pall Mall Magazine*, vii, September 1895.
5. R. A. Gregory, *Nature*, 10 February 1898.

6. Yevgeni Zamayatin, *H. G. Wells*, 1922, reprinted in *A Soviet Heretic*, trans. Mirra Ginsburg, University of Chicago Press, 1970, pp. 260–61.

7. Antonina Vallentin, *H. G. Wells: Prophet of Our Day*, trans. Daphne Woodward, John Day 1950, p. 106.

8. V. S. Pritchett, *The Living Novel*, Chatto & Windus 1946, p. 117.

9. J. B. Priestley, introduction to *The War of the Worlds*, Easton Press 1964.

10. George Orwell, *The True Pattern of H. G. Wells*, Manchester Evening News, 14 August 1946.

11. Vincent Brome, *H. G. Wells: A Biography*, Longman 1952, pp. 64–5.

12. Bernard Bergonzi, *The Early H. G. Wells*, M.U.P. 1961, p. 61.

13. Norman and Jeanne Mackenzie, *The Time Traveller*, Weidenfeld & Nicolson 1973, p. 120.

14. Anthony West, *H. G. Wells: Aspects of a Life*, Random House 1984, p. 226.

15. Michael Moorcock, introduction to *The Time Machine*, Everyman 1994, p. xxxvi.

16. Malcolm Muggeridge, *The Thirties*, Fontana 1971, p. 35 (first pub. 1940). Pauline Kael, writing many years after Muggeridge, takes much the same line over the pseudo-Greek look of the film, and call Wells's screeplay 'tendentious', but dubs the film 'the most elaborate' sci-fi made in England until Arthur C. Clarke's *2001*.

17. Herbert Read, *English Prose Style*, Bell 1928, p.146.

18. Raymond Williams, *The English Novel*, Paladin 1974, pp. 98–9, 102–3, 104.

19. Kingsley Martin, *Editor*, Penguin 1969, pp. 101–2.

SUGGESTIONS FOR FURTHER READING

Criticism and Biography

Bergonzi, Bernard, *The Early H. G. Wells*, M.U.P. 1961

Brome, Vincent, *H. G. Wells: A Biography*, Longman 1951

Carey, John, *The Intellectuals and the Masses*, Faber & Faber 1992

Dickson, Lovat, *H. G. Wells: His Turbulent Life and Times*, Penguin 1972

Haynes, Rosslyn D., *H. G. Wells: Discoverer of the Future*, N.Y.U.P. 1980

Hynes, Samuel, *The Edwardian Turn of Mind*, Oxford 1968

Mackenzie, Norman and Jeanne, *The Time Traveller*, Weidenfeld & Nicolson 1973

Pritchett, V. S., *The Living Novel*, Chatto & Windus 1946

Smith, David. C., *H. G. Wells: Desperately Mortal*, Yale 1983

Swinnerton, Frank, *The Georgian Literary Scene*, Hutchinson 1935

West, Anthony, *Aspects of a Life*, Random House 1984

West, Geoffrey, *H. G. Wells: Sketch for a Portrait*, Norton 1930

Williams, Raymond, *The Country and the City*, Paladin 1975

Background

Darwin, *The Origin of Species*, ed. J. W. Burrow, Penguin 1982

Gaarder, Jostein, *Sophie's World* (Chapter on Darwin), Phoenix House, 1995

Glendinning, Victoria, *Electricity*, Hutchinson 1995

Gould, Stephen Jay, *Bully for Brontosaurus* (Ch. 8), Penguin 1991

Hobsbawm, Eric, *The Age of Capital* (Ch. 14), Abacus 1975

Irvine, William, *Apes, Angles & Victorians*, Weidenfeld 1955

Levin, Bernard, *A World Elsewhere*, Cape 1994

Morris, William, *News from Nowhere*, Chatto & Windus 1912

Mumford, Lewis, *The Story of Utopias*, Boni & Liveright 1922

Wells, H. G., *The Outline of History* (revised edition, Ch. 37 §5 and §6), Cassell 1951

Wells, H. G., *Experiment in Autobiography*, Faber & Faber 1984

Williams, Raymond, *Keywords*, Fontana 1976

TEXT SUMMARY

Chapter One
The Time Traveller, Psychologist, Medical Man, Provincial Mayor, Very Young Man, Filby and the Narrator discuss the existence and nature of a fourth dimension; the Time Traveller experiments with a miniature time machine and shows his guests the full-size version he is building.

Chapter Two
The Psychologist, Journalist, Editor, Silent Man, Medical Man and Narrator gather at the Time Traveller's, but he is not there. He appears, dishevelled and lame, and begins his story.

Chapter Three
The Time Traveller tells of his sensations as he travelled through time, and of the creatures he saw when he and his machine halted.

Chapter Four
The Time Traveller dines with the creatures he has met; he comments on their nature and way of life and considers how the world of his own time could have changed to that in which he now finds himself.

Chapter Five
The Time Traveller discovers his machine has disappeared. He meets Weena; he also catches glimpses of creatures other than those he first met and concludes there are two distinct peoples, those who live above ground, and those who exist below.

Chapter Six
Convinced the under-world creatures – Morlocks – have taken his machine, the Time Traveller descends to their underground caverns but has to escape, empty-handed.

Chapter Seven
Like the upper-worlders – the Eloi – the Time Traveller comes to fear the dark; he also loathes the Morlocks. He considers the relationship between the two races and realizes that the once-subservient Morlocks now dominate the Eloi. He takes Weena to explore a large palace but it is further than he thought and, with darkness approaching, his and Weena's fear of the Morlocks grows. They spend the night safely, but the Time Traveller resolves to devise a way to ward off the under-worlders.

Chapter Eight
In the large palace, which turns out to be a ruined museum, the Time Traveller finds matches, camphor and a metal bar to use against the Morlocks.

Chapter Nine
Returning from the museum, the Time Traveller and Weena are forced through tiredness to rest in a forest. Although the Time Traveller has set fire to the trees to fend off the Morlocks, the two are attacked and Weena disappears. The Morlocks, however, are blinded by the raging fire.

Chapter Ten
The Time Traveller returns to the Eloi and finds his time machine. The Morlocks attempt to trap him, but he escapes.

Chapter Eleven
The Time Traveller goes on through the future to discover a cold, almost lifeless earth with a dying sun.

Chapter Twelve
Returning to his own time, the Time Traveller is greeted with scepticism. The Narrator visits him again, but he disappears.

Epilogue
The Time Traveller never returns and the Narrator reflects on what might have befallen him; he also considers his own view of the future.